Dancing Out Of Covid

Also by Jim Gold

Journals

A New Leaf: Adventures in the Creative Life (Vols. 1–5)

A New Leaf: Adventures in the Creative Life (Selected Edition)

Dancing Through Covid (Journals 2019–2022)

Fiction

Mad Shoes: The Adventures of Sylvan Woods

Handfuls of Air: Stories and Poems

Crusader Tours

Zany! A Father–Son Odyssey

Carlos the Cloud and Other Stories

Choreography

A Treasury of International Folk Dances: A Step-by-Step Guide

Dancing Out Of Covid

JOURNALS 2022–2023

Full Court Press
Englewood Cliffs, New Jersey

First Edition

Copyright © 2023 by Jim Gold

All rights reserved. No part of this book may be
reproduced or transmitted in any form or by any means electronic
or mechanical, including by photocopying,
by recording, or by any information storage and retrieval system,
without the express permission of the author,
except where permitted by law.

Published in the United States of America
by Full Court Press, 601 Palisade Avenue,
Englewood Cliffs, NJ 07632
fullcourtpress.com

ISBN 978-1-953728-18-0
Library of Congress Control No. 2023916774

Editing and book design by Barry Sheinkopf

For Bernice
Always and ever

Table of Contents

Chapter 1
Psychological Travel, *3*

Chapter 2
Performing in the New Neighborhood, *33*

Chapter 3
The Moderate Life, *69*

Chapter 4
Childhood Revisited, *103*

Chapter 5
Belief Works, *115*

Chapter 6
Stranger Than Fiction: Love and Helping Others, *115*

Chapter 7
Postscript, *135*

Chapter 8
Performance Life Workbook, *141*

CHAPTER ONE

Psychological Travel

Monday, November 28, 2022
Return to Tours

I'm re-entering the tour business on a different level. Anxieties and upsets have drifted away—ghosts fading fast—and through awareness may soon drop out on their own. Responsibilities are ripening into satisfaction.

I'm upgrading my tour web pages. Plus I love the big checks. Doing it the way I love brings joy and glory.

Sunday, December 4, 2022
I Suffer, But So What?

> I suffer, but so what?
> Tight muscles tighten the screws
> Forcing me to remember
> Healing myself comes first
> When I do, others may follow.

Acting Practice

Performing is an act.   Act well.

Who Am I?

If I am always on stage, giving a show, what about the inner me? Who am I? Inner and outer, private and public, I am both. *They* are the real me"   All is One.

Wednesday, December 7, 2022

Losing in politics hurts my ego. Lose, lose, lose, is political agony: just as artistic agony is *not* creating, just as winning is political ecstasy, and artistic ecstasy *is* the act of creating.

What to do? Dive right in. Never stop. Never give up.

If this is the rule, why bother dwelling on agony, or even ecstasy? Both extremes lead to downfalls. Rather, say hello to the neighbors, then pass them by. Dive straight in to the performing life.

What is the proper reaction to discouragement?

Drop the collapse. Get mad at myself instead for giving up.

Visiting the Numb-Dumb Monastery

Numb fingers are dumb fingers. They cannot write or play.

What is the purpose of this cervical breakdown? Why did my fingers become numb? Why are they *still* stiff, paralyzed, and speechless? Evidently, I need to leave the Numb-Dumb Monastery, take some free time to meditate, space to re-examine direction.

My fingers need to write and play guitar.

Writing

Private equals public, and both equal performance. This idea makes my journal writing very important! People should read my journals. Although few may, does it really matter? Sure, I would love it; my ego would be soothed and happy. But as for quality, it really doesn't matter. Readership numbers have nothing to do with importance.

I'm glad I'm finally thinking this way.

Are Numb Thoughts Dumb Thoughts?

Finger numbness frees me from the fear of performing on the classical guitar. Numbness distracts me; distraction is my numbness.

Would I be free to play without these symptoms?

I don't know.

But note: Without symptoms to protect and motivate me, would I *ever* play guitar? Truth is, beyond them lies an even greater terror of the grand emptiness, the vacuum of no purpose. So numbness distracts me from performing fright, which distracts me from the vacuum. Lots of distractions here.

But without all these performing anxieties, who am I? What am I? What would I do without them? I'm hoping that by jumping into the vacuum, I will find reasons like fun, freedom, and even a great and glorious laugh. (Note: The numbness in my fingers has now shifted to my lower back.)

Thursday, December 8, 2022

I'm happy about last night's numbness revelations. This morning it has mostly dissolved, vanished into the vacuum. I'm ready to swim in the great waters of gaida-glory laugher. The curtain has lifted.

Dwell not on the ecstasy but how to move beyond it into the performing life. Start with my usual morning hour of Hebrew study. Enjoy what little finger numbness is left. Watch it dwindle as it flails along, ever trying to distract me from the vacuum. I wag a warning finger at it: "You can't fool me anymore."

Friday, December 9, 2022
Hallelujah Hands: Another Success Story

Empty, dry, no juice, flow, dreams, or effort. Motivation zero. Sounds like I've given up.

Yes, I have lost the self-beating guitar whip, the chain tying me to my private gravestone. Nothing is beating me up anymore. I miss my personal tormentors. The flying devils hanging around my classical guitar brain kept me busy night and day, whipping me into a guitar-practice frenzy. I mourn their exit and feel a bit lost without them.

Indeed, without my Supreme Beater, I feel disoriented, spiritless. It's a big loss, but one I've wanted for years. Now that I've lost it, I've achieved success, a big one: But although glorious in itself, is followed by the "now what?" stage with its feelings of sadness and loss of direction.

As I step onto the performing life stage, it feels like a bright chapter is beginning. With Audience Beaters and Public Critics diminished, even out of sight, *I am free to flow.*

I'm not used to such freedom. Who or what will motivate me? They say that love, passion, curiosity, and fascination do the job. But do they? Let's see if these potential mates work. I know their extremes are an illusion fostered by stupidity. The golden mean is true. Seeing both sides fosters smarts and wisdom. So my classical guitar self-beating attitude has been stupid. By embracing the new Performing Life, I am moving from stupid to smart.

Hallelujah Hands Conclusion

It's stimulating to seek excellence. Seeking it is my self-motivation platform. But did my self-beating confer any advantages? Well, it brought high standards. I beat myself to reach them. I want to keep high standards but give up self-beating. *Or do I?* I don't want these standards to paralyze me and stop my ascent. How to do that?

The truth is that pushing, self-beating into the abyss, is a victory. Time to accept jubilation.

Saturday, December 10, 2022

Everything feels screwed up and broken. Sure. It's just a feeling, but it's there. Anger doesn't work anymore. It's not the turn-on it used to be. I mourn the loss of its energy. With rage gone, its power diminishing—a dying light. Are there any replacements in sight? What about love and beauty? Can they ever have such striking power? I hope so.

Release of the Humor Dragon

My self-discipline has *also* disappeared, drifting away along with self-beating. I need that discipline. I've had it all my life.

Do I still *want* it, though? Not in the familiar way. I want to keep the freedom but add a new form of self-discipline to it. That's the next level I'm looking for.

Enthusiasm and spark are found in miracles. So I must bind myself to my miracle schedule again. But it's broken, at least for now. Humor uplifts my mind, takes me out of the present, rockets my brain into a sparkling stratosphere. Can I find discipline in the humor realm?

Dare I try humor in folk tour, book promotions, or ads? If I use it in business and it fails, will my business be destroyed? On the other hand, what is more important, business as usual or taking a chance on self-growth? Humor is a risk worth taking.

Sunday, December 11, 2022
Confidence and Humor

I'm building a new foundation based on numb fingers and humor. Through their erosion of my old performing attitude, numb fingers have become the gateway to confidence; their handmaiden is humor.

Part of funny classical guitar playing may be the "numbed" (relaxed) left hand, where *many* notes are muffled, even left out. If *most* of the notes were muffled or left out, that might be even funnier.

Even daring to do such a thing is sacrilege. Not to play guitar clearly (and perfectly) is, in itself, at best, a mistake, an error to be scorned, but at worst, and in classical guitar reality, a sacrilege! Johann Sebastian Bach is an icon, a god. By messing up his compositions, I am mistreating a god. Indeed, making such a musical and tonal mess of his "Gavotte in D," along with the "Musette," is *utter* sacrilege! . . . But sacrilege can be funny, too.

As a folk singer, would I dare sing "Down in the Dungeon," "Mule Skinners Blues," or "Rock Island Line" and be so imperfect? Maybe. Could messy and imperfect be my new voice? *Wailin' Jim and his Messy Guitar.* Throw in the gaida, and I've got a *real* mess. Maybe that's the title of my new comedy show.

Tuesday, December 13, 2022
Loving my Business

Are my mathematical and organizational skills important work? Are they worthwhile, filled with purpose and meaning?

I see my past answering: "According to your love-of-artist background, the answer is no. Only art is worthy. Everything else is lower, not as important. Art rises above everything. The artist is the closest thing to god we can find on this earth."

Having been brought up in this atmosphere, I agreed—until today, when the subjects of mathematics and organizational ability came in my tour business. I'm fairly good at math and organizing, even though, in my mind, I toss it off as "nothing." But they're not *nothing*. They're something. They're gifts from the Big Guy. By downplaying them, I downplay myself and Him as well. And of course, dismiss all the fun, satisfaction, and joy of succeeding in business!

Thursday, December 15, 2022
Duty to Perform

Performing can bring anxiety. But make peace with the anxiety, and watch the numbness disappear. It has no choice but to vanish. If I choose to grab the serpent by the neck and perform, impediment and disability will not stop me. Yes, I may play poorly, make lots of mistakes, but at least I'm in the fight.

Showing up is the point. Folk dance with a limp. So what? Low to no tour registrations? Business continues. Computer stiff neck? Stretch more. Embarrassment? Blush with pleasure. Bring them on. By making peace with my burdens, diving into noxious necessary tasks, sealing myself in responsibilities, I'm ready to roll.

The Truth of Warming Up

Warm-ups are a mental thing. Does the body need to warm up, if the mind is hot? Yes. Through mental imaging, jump quickly into the passion. Let it burn. Start with one "Gavotte" note. Then on to the next.

Accepting Limits: Shining in a Good Place

I can do only so much with my limited talents. However, they can still go far. They have their place. And it's a good place. I can play "Sor Etude No. 12" slowly. And it has its place. Somewhere. It's a good place, too. Only perhaps "different" from the traditional fast one.

The good place is that I can perform anywhere, in anything, and on anything. And that I *do* perform anywhere, in, and on anything! It's that, now, I can live comfortably, happily, in my performing life.

Numb to Criticism

I have numbed my fingers to criticism. Perhaps that is the meaning of my numbness. Note how it has freed me for the performing life.

Since everything I do belongs to performance, even playing the "Sor Etude No. 12" slowly, very slowly, very very slowly, *infinitesimally* slow, is a performance. No need to rush. I am there already. As soon as I start, I am there. In fact, I am there even before I start—and it all belongs to performance. Even the electric crackling in my left hand fingers is part of it. Numbness itself is part of it.

It's a slow re-entry because I have to get used to this new way of thinking about everything I do, no matter how I do it. *There's no rush. Slow is part of the show.*

The Obelisk

The obelisk of classical guitar performance has punctured the balloon of energy above it, and all the energy has poured out, flooding the plains, mountains, and countryside of the entire earth, making things grow equally in all-is-one performing importance.

The opposites slow/fast, good/bad, and more have all disappeared, submerged under a sea of energy—a performance synthesis.

Saturday, December 17, 2022
Fear, Anger, Curiosity, the Unknown: Four Great Motivators

I start out with Freedom, which flattens my choices into *anything*, and Duty, the dive-in path of *performance*. The Duty road is the only one. Riding on it, I drive past the pillars of Death and Immortality, realizing they are beside the point. I am free to choose the Duty road or float among the clouds of freedom. I can choose either whenever I "feel like it," which means whenever I am motivated to do so.

But as the soft breezes blow, what will motivate me? My friends Fear and Anger? Can I generate them at will, especially when I have nothing to fear or be angry about?

I like Fear and Anger. They are effective generation tools. Anything else? How about Curiosity? And especially The Unknown?

Indeed, these four are incredible motivating tools. They jump-start your journey, put you immediately on the Duty Road.

The four Great Motivators: Fear, Anger, Curiosity, Unknown. FACU (Fack You). A memorable acronym.

No Hebrew this morning. I'm focusing on absorbing the above message. Especially its Curiosity and Unknown aspects. Could they supplant Fear and Anger for me? Does the Unknown, aka Mother Unknown Universe, create the earthly motivators Fear, Anger, and Curiosity? I'd say Yes.

This means recognizing and then acknowledging post-numb-finger motivators entering my New Performance Life.

First came the Cervical Thruway, with those numb fingers, destroying the old traumatic life. Then came the transition—slow healing of neck and fingers. And finally, today's Curiosity and Unknown motivators stepped into the picture. This puts me on a firmer foundation.

Rough or Smooth Ride

In general, motivators and motivation are good things. Nevertheless, some motivators create a rough or "negative" ride while others create a smooth or "positive" one.

I'd call Fear and Anger "negative" motivators; they served mostly in my old neighborhood. On the other hand, Curiosity and the Unknown are now my "positive" motivational stars. Will Fear and Anger diminish as Curiosity and the Unknown step in? I think that would be lovely. But strangely unimaginable.

On the other hand, I wonder if this thought is realistic, or even good? Do I really want to lose, give up my old friends, drop them completely? After all, they served me well, did lots of good things for me. And it's not a good idea to dump old friends.

Yet I do want and need to move on.

Is there some way we can still all work together? My financial fears have diminished. Not much reason for them, at least in their old intense form. Anger, mostly directed at my responsibilities, has also faded. Not much reason for it—at least in its former intensity, either.

So maybe flowing with Curiosity and the Unknown as fresh motivators is my next step. It's anyhow stupid, naive, and unrealistic to think Fear and Anger will ever go away. Perhaps they will endure in their diminished forms, along with Curiosity, as I enter the Unknown.

This means I "know" too much, which actually means I am traveling down known pathways—doing only, or mainly, things I know how to do. This opens the door to boredom.

Unknown pathways foster curiosity. Perhaps it's time to move into that. The post-Covid period is ending. With the coming of 2023, it may, for me, be completely over.

Sunday, December 18, 2022
Serious Side

A Sarnoian TMS numb-finger entry: My fingers will stay numb until I find a new reason to play guitar.

With the initial publication, and, weeks later, yesterday's email promotion of *Dancing Through Covid*, the serious side of me is being revealed in public. A major personal step. Along with the birth of a gone-public-serious side I may find a new reason to play guitar! In the past, by refusing to acknowledge my serious side, steering away from the uncomfortable feeling of revealing it in public, I can explain my attitude as *having been numb to my serious side*. But now, through publication and promotion of the new book, my serious side has revealed itself.

Quite a shock.

But here is a new possibility: Serious writing and serious classical guitar can merge there.

My serious side is my suffering side.

Classical music has always expressed suffering under the squeeze, awe, wonder, and magnificent meltdown from its Beethovian Beauty. Classical music contains the artistic nobility of suffering and its agony-and-ecstasy path.

I believe with absolute certainty that the numbness and tingling in my fingers are my serious side, my suffering side, breaking through their protective private walls.

My numbness and tingling are TMS at its best.

A possible upcoming result: A serious reason to play classical guitar may soon be born.

Fear of giving concerts was (partly) due to fear that my serious side would be revealed in public. (This would mean showing I am "weak," and humiliation would follow. How I arrived at such a conclusion can only be explained by my upbringing. Somehow, by suffering, I show weakness. According to my family mythology, only laughing, smiling people are cool winners. Sufferers are losers. That's why they suffer.

Ridiculous, crazy, but that's the way I grew up.

Truth is, I know and believe only *smart* people suffer. The dumb remain in blissful ignorant laughter.

And artists suffer the most! This may seem self-serving and arrogant. But it's true. The deeply felt agony and ecstasy make it so.

So, all in all, the curtain is lifting. My serious side is here. A sleeping bear has awoken. Classical guitar will use its paw to slap and crush all resistance.

The numbing and tingling of nerves in my hands are the giant bear stirring. As left hand fingers unfold, classical guitar-playing power wakens.

My serious side is my power side. No more slap-downs.

Retirement

I'm not retiring. Artists and entrepreneurs never retire. In fact, I'm working harder than ever. Only, looking back, why did I distract myself with a cervical neck problem, its subsequent finger numbness, and an inability to play guitar? True, in the beginning, I was happy to take a rest. But that ended quickly. Perhaps it was because the power scared me. Especially mine. By liberating myself from the albatross of performance, I released a flood of freedom, potential chaos, and inner strength.

I got scared. What would I do with all that power? Would it destroy me?

So I distracted myself with a TMS "solution."

But now I've stepped outside of my tingle-numb house. It's over. I'm on to another location.

Now I marvel at my left hand burning-to-break-out torch.

I even understand why I "like" to walk around the house a bit stooped and hunched over. In doing so, I am "happily" revisiting the former neighborhood, taking a break from my power by denying it, by being small, weak, and hunched over again.

But this is all ending. My power is now out there with the appearance of *Dancing Through Covid,* for all my email list to see.

Tingle away, old friend! Your days are over.

Work-It-Through Process: Serious Side Offers Serious Fun

The classical guitar work-it-through process may take a month . . .or more. . .or less.

But it starts today. Luckily, there's no rush. Let's do some serious suffering—touch of humor included. Can humor do that? Why not? It's freeing and fun. My serious side can have some.

Monday, December 19, 2022
Return: I Hate It, But. . .

Is that what 2023 is all about? Probably.

I had "decided" never to perform on classical guitar again, never again to give a concert. I felt free and victorious. But a cervical collapse, along with numb fingers, followed almost immediately. What did this mean? That something was wrong with my decision. Freeing myself from performing fear by abandoning my "goal" of some day giving a concert was really more threatening than the perhaps unrealizable goal of giving the concert itself.

I needed the energy and motivation of that fear to guide and lead me forward, into the future, wherever and whatever that might be. That *positive fear of performing* has been a vicious friend of mine for years, maybe for my entire life. Giving it up, abandoning its direction, means death.

The TMS message of numb fingers is now clear to me: The goal of someday performing a concert of classical guitar is not an albatross around my neck, pushing me to the ground, sinking my dreams in fear. Rather, it is an eagle pushing me to soar. Its wings are the energy and motivation it gives me.

Sink or soar? Crippled and limping with an empty tank, go down, crash with the albatross, or, using the fuel of positive fear, fly with the eagle? Is there even a choice?

I have to perform! There is no alternative. . .but death.

You can't soar without fear. But when you do, ecstasy, with all its endorphins, comes along for the ride. So, like Tara the Stonecutter, I'm back to where I started. After three years of living in the Monastery of Covid Retreat, collecting and reevaluating all my thoughts, it's time to re-enter and move ahead.

I cannot and will never retire. I will re-enter as an older, wiser, new species of post-Covid man.

Again

After all, my journal is now called *The Performing Life*. I am ready. Time to jump off the cliff, dive into the abyss. (Holding back only means dying in the process.) Does this mean I have to lead tours again? Maybe. Does it mean giving concerts, doing bookings? Maybe. Evidently, I need the positive fear of performance. Yes, it scares the hell out of me. But as Sartre put it, *No Exit*. No other way.

Benefits of Performing

Feeling alone, as opposed to *being* alone, is the illusion curse of separation.

Performing for others is really a service for and to them. It lifts me out of the aloneness of self into an egoless state.

Guitar: The Light(er)-Touch Guitar Technique

The electric shock in my left hand does herald a much lighter way of pressing on the guitar neck.

On the optimistic side, my left-hand fingers pressing lightly on the fingerboard lead to lighter guitar playing, which could lead to a *lighter approach to classical guitar.* A plus.

This would be new for me.

Light Pressing

Try it with scales, barres, my guitar pieces, etc.

As I play G scale rapidly in the second position, the nerves, corpuscles, and cells in my left hand are all breaking down in an explosion of electric nerve shock. Maybe the old must be destroyed before the new can enter and take its place.

Also, could this be my introduction to the old dream of fast guitar playing? It certainly is easier and faster when you hardly press left hand fingers on the fingerboard. Such light pressing creates muffled, muted notes, formerly called "sloppy."

Is such "sloppy" playing an entrance to a new guitar technique? Is it part of my freedom road? What implications does such "light pressing" have for my legs and folk dancing? For exercise?

Does it explain being "tired" in the gym yesterday and the past few days? Am I on the cusp of a *technique*?

Does "tired" open the door, lead to, and mean a lighter touch attitude in general, a not-push-so-hard attitude in life?

Wednesday, December 21, 2022
Deep Diving

There's nothing I have to do anymore: finished, done, complete. No need for practicing to improve or competing to be best.

I'm free to spend my time diving in and Diving Deep.

Suffering

Why do I suffer? Why do we all? It could be what makes us human. The difference between animals and humans is that, while both feel pain, only humans suffer because they are aware of mortality. Are animals aware of mortality? Ask them.

Stick to the Path

Philosophy and art merge in guitar suffering. The pain is expressed through my right hand. But today my *left* hand fingers feel numb, to which add hypothenar electric nerve shocks. Slow, thoughtful, focused playing stops the shocks. Why is this happening?

My performing obsession has been broken: I no longer have to play in public! Breaking these ancient chains, though, brings the chaos of freedom. Ontological terror strikes my fingers. Numb and void, they tingle with nerve shocks.

The lock on Pandora's box of inhibitions has been broken, and freedom is running wild. This untamed stallion will destroy my guitar playing, and more. It must be stopped. Rein it in with discipline. Focus the mind.

Friday, December 23, 2022

Here's the real question in editing my journal: Is what I am reading helpful in daily life?

Best All-Is-One Combo

The best dream is the All-Is-One dream.
To sleep and wake up with it brings a bountiful morning.

Guitar: Maximum Lightness

Get back to the sheer pleasure of plucking at any speed.

Learn maximum left-hand lightness: *hardly press the strings.* Benefits: Maximum lightness in the left hand, when achieved through intense focus, eliminates all nerve shocks and finger numbness. It improves flow and makes the sensuality of speed a pleasure.

Saturday, December 24, 2022
Inspirational: The Teacher Comes

At the gym I see Chris struggling, pushing hard, trying with all his screaming might to grow his muscle and improve his strength. Pain and focus in action.

What is the attraction of suffering? Somehow I want to heal his pain. I won't be whole again until I do. I'm also a bit jealous. Jealousy is a good sign. It means I want it for myself. What do I want? The power of his focus. And focus can be painful. As agony is often the route to ecstasy, and pain the bridge to focus and strength. No avoiding pain: Dive into the struggle; focus will emerge, followed by defeats, but also victories, pride, and glory.

Sunday, December 25, 2022
Morning Hebrew Study

Focus on each word becomes a method becomes a meditation. Quantitative change leads to qualitative change. Less leads to slower leads to more self-control. And with self control comes power. A good thing.

Giving Up My Guitar Dreams (Or Are They Nightmares?

Perhaps the purpose of "Alhambra" has been to teach me *how to play slowly!* To give up aiming to play fast. Perhaps it is not a wise or healthy goal. And to accept this wisdom. Focus on the *moment. Patience.*

If this is true, it means giving up my dream of playing fast, changing it from fast to slow. Such thinking could free me and be a blessing!

Inspiration

I read history for ideas and inspiration. How about reading my *own* history—my journals, stories, and other writing? I need to be inspired not only by the past of others, but by my past as well.

Monday, December 26, 2022
Motivation

My source of motivation is self-improvement. Once it starts, enthusiasm spreads, and soon the flames reach out, warming on-lookers with touches of inspiration. Soon, fields are on fire, weeds burn, and new stalks sprout forth.

When Covid's putridity began its destruction, I descended into a maelstrom of business collapse, internal examination, and attitude re-evaluation. During this blind spin, the gem of self-improvement knowledge slipped into darkness.

Now, almost three years later, negative attitudes have been washed away, replaced by upbeat new ones. Self-improvement, coupled with love and virtue, appears once more before my dreaming eyes.

A renaissance reason to practice guitar: To improve! That's it. Of course, along with getting better, like Johann Sebastian Bach, also play for the glory of God. But during this crisis time, sinking beneath the poisoned Covid river of sudden change. I had forgotten this truth.

Bathed in its glory, I again shine with wonder and purpose. Happy vibrations have returned.

Loosening Out

My guitar playing is loosening up—and loosening out. I'm in a flying regime. Modes of travel along the Graveyard Path fell into desuetude; littered with trash, broken stones, and boredom, they rolled away.

Time to dispel the doubt monster, say goodbye to Mr. Question Mark, and Mrs. Am-I-Wrong. Let their gray hesitations and lurid doubts be buried.

Loosening out, down, and up all work together, guiding the heated soul on the upward path, creating celestial travel at its best.

A ride on that road fills your heart with victor's blood. You arrive at destinations brave and strong. In fact, being on it makes daring beside the point.

Tuesday, December 27, 2022
Why Not Stay Home?

If space and time do not exist, and we are all connected on the deepest spiritual level, why leave the house? Why not stay home? What's the big deal whether I meet people in person or not? We're all connected anyway. Why not just stay in place and listen to the unity beat? Everyone wants love and connection.

What is love *but* connection.

So since we're all connected, why not stay home and meditate on realizing it? Spend your time focusing on *connection*. What's the big deal?

That's all I have to do. . .forever—perform this small but monumental task. Is it really so hard?

Wednesday, December 28, 2022
Audience Inspiration Land

Audience as a positive force inspires me to make my best effort. I am stepping gently, totally, quietly, easily, and naturally into Audience Inspiration land. This is my *real home.*

Most amazing is how little effort it took to get here. Seems like I just "fell into it," like the last autumn leaf falls off a tree. (Of course, this *is* the autumn of my life, so maybe the simile is a good one.) It's my Performance Life home of love and inspiration. Maybe that's why it feels so easy and natural.

Guitar

I'm meditating on the rebirth of each finger in the audience inspiration mode. The electric-shock pinpricks in my left-hand fingers dignify a separation from audience inspiration. So does the numbness in my fingers.

Clearly, I can't rush the transition: slow and steady on the road of cracks.

But I *can* feel glory in the *wonder of transition* along the way. There is nothing to say to others about this. The fireworks are all an internal show, for my benefit alone.

Playful Am I

I like to play with failure, fool around with it. But I know success. It has a serious side. Can glory and playfulness be combined?

Why not?

Should they be?

Why not? I just have to *decide* on it and make it so. (Of course, paradoxically, the split between them itself is playful, thus glorious.) This means there is no getting away from glory.

But I want to be inclusive. Even misery and pain are, then, part of that glory—only a lower part.

Old Friends

Pain and misery play their parts in my theater of the world. I create them as part of my acting team.

Do I want to keep both as playmates? I keep *inviting* them into my playground.

As old friends, we have a long history together. Is it fair to just drop them, kick them out? Is that a way to treat old friends, even lousy ones? Of course, glory, magnificence, and beauty are also old friends. I keep inviting *them* into my playground, too. And all my old friends play together. They all help me have a good time in their own way. Does it really matter how?

Thursday, December 29, 2022
Another Look at Alhambra

"Alhambra" is perhaps my greatest and best put-down tool. I can, and do always play it to discourage myself. And it succeeds almost every time! Then I add general classic guitar playing, along with the subtle, old-time classical music message, *I'll never be able to get it right*, to continue discouraging myself.

How paradoxical: the "Alhambra," a composition I love and that inspired me to play classical guitar, is my downfall piece, my instrument of discouragement.

But perhaps I should look at my original reasons for even wanting to play classical guitar: So I could prove to my audience that I was worthy, good enough, and, if I could prove it by playing a few classical guitar pieces well, in the beginning of my show, then I was free to release myself (my *true* self?) in song, humor, stories, wild group singing, off-beat group interactions, and crazy off-the-wall stuff.

In other words, I started classical guitar lessons, not really for love, but as a confidence crutch, a shield against audience criticism, and to prove myself worthy.

So maybe I really hated the piece I loved—or rather, hated the reasons I had to play it, and classical guitar in general. (Note: I had no trouble with *flamencan* guitar. But that is "folk music".)

I should give up my reasons for playing "Alhambra" and classical guitar. I'm ready, willing, and able. And until I get my brain and attitude together, should I give them both up, at least temporarily? Does this mean, if I had my life to live over, I'd be a folk singer? Maybe.

But one of this life's tasks was to remove my lack of confidence. That's why classical guitar was bestowed on me. Classical music also gave me my love of *all* music. And due to the block, I was "forced" to develop my folk dance and organizational skills. Through these in turn came Folk Dance Tours, Folk Dance Weekends, even classes. Indeed, there were *benefits* to the confidence blockage I lived with.

So maybe, next life I'll be a folk singer. We'll see.

On the long-range positive side, I could I say I mobilized the classical guitar and "Alhambra" blockage to divert my energy stream. I was "forced" to diversify, develop other talents, skills, interests, explore other sides of my personality.

Frightening thought: Does this mean that "Alhambra" and classical guitar have now served their purpose? I no longer need or want to put myself down. I've left that behind. Classical guitar music was never thrilling and beloved like the violin. But it was a helluva *status* thing, gave me a competitive performing edge, and was thus worthy. Does this mean I give them up and move on? No question I'm ready to. But to what?

Another frightening question: If I no longer need classical guitar or stock market trading, what will I do with all this free time?

Maybe I should continue to do my stuff simply because I have nothing better to do, because doing something is better than doing nothing. And maybe nothing better is what I do best.

Good or bad, for better or worse, I'm putting a moral value on time and action.

Friday, December 30, 2022
Just do it!

Totally in the present. But what if, in this here and now, I feel like shit and lack the desire to do anything? Do it anyway. Just do it! Slowly, slowly the ship sails through the fog.

Saturday, December 31, 2022
The Search: Wanted—Fresh, Dynamic, Challenging

I woke up this morning with terrible hypothenar pain in my *left* hand. Why, I don't know.

Certainly, it helps disable my guitar playing.

This morning, I feel disabled in general. Strange, but I am not unhappy with this feeling. It encourages me stay home, out of the limelight, and never leave the house again to "go to work." (Of course, except for folk dancing teaching and folk tour organization, I don't *have* any work.)

Will this disabling attitude be part of my New Year's return to society? Does it speak of a big change, or at least a shift, in my life?

Truth is, after training for two years in Covid lock-downs, a good part of me now *likes* to stay home! I enjoy my solitude and freedom along with occasional visits with friends, sessions with my trainer, and trips to the gym.

I hate to say it, but it's not a bad life at all. Yesterday started off with a "just do it" bang. Today I ask: "Just do what?"

Could I even be tired of the responsibility of teaching folk dancing? Has it become "work" and run its course?

Or am I just tired and lazy?

Or clearing the path for a new attitude and way of life?

Maybe it is a bit of all three. "Lazy" means I'm getting tired of the old. "Sleepy and old" mean I'm looking for rebirth. No better time than a New Year.

Dropping folk dance teaching and tours would sure be dramatic and novel. And today I'd love to take that adventure.

Interesting I should say this. And since I've brought it up, let me explore it. Based on today's sentiments, dropping all my folk dance and tour responsibilities seems lovely. Imagine a blank slate, a fresh start and clear road staring me in the face. Just for fun, let's imagine I have it. Now what?

The working New Year begins Tuesday morning. What would I have to look forward to? Dealing and trading in the stock market. Anything else? Can't think of a thing. Are stocks the only fresh, dynamic, and challenging thing I have left in my life? Maybe. Note those words. Evidently, these are motivational triggers I need in my life. But as of today, except for trading stocks, nothing fills the bill. I haven't found it yet.

Sunday, January 1, 2023
New Year, and a New Year's Resolution

Is the belief that the soul lives forever a truth or a choice? Does it really live forever? There is no way to prove it, scientific or otherwise. No one knows for sure.

Sure, the body leaves (Wayne Dyer), falls away, is discarded. But is there an invincible remnant, an eternal part, that endures?

As a lifstyle, it is better, more optimistic and cheerful, to believe there is. To "know" some of you lives forever encourages the feeling of invincibility, which gives you courage and infinite hope.

Of course. I realize the physical body will fade and eventually disappear. Frightening indeed. But believing part of you will go on is heartening and wonderful.

Since no one knows for sure, a belief system is a choice. It can be a conscious choice, coming through study and personal hopes, or an "unconscious" choice, coming through upbringing, religious practices, societal influences, and external, outside forces.

But whether it's a choice or not, believing I am part of an eternal soul, that part of me will go on forever, comes as a real relief.

So why not choose invincibility over disappearance? It's such a good feeling. And if the truth of the matter lies only in your choice. . .then why not choose the positive, wonderful, happy belief? I'd sure like that. I'd even say I need it.

Such a focus would help me modulate doubt, which, although sometimes important, is often a killer attitude.

Focus on the will also gives me a feeling of invincibility. I sure could use such an upbeat feeling as I plan the rest of my life.

Improvement

Could wanting and working to "improve" myself actually make things worse?

Practicing "Alhambra" in order to improve my rendition has never made it better. (I think I played it better when I first learned it years ago!) After years of practice, it hasn't changed much at all. Maybe it has even gotten worse.

And constantly failing proves I'm not a good enough guitarist.

How could I, if at all, play it today? As a start (and perhaps a finish), I'd need an *invincible* "Alhambra."

Monday, January 2, 2023
New Year Crystallization: The Fun of Stress

In spite of frailty and weakness, limps, thumb pains, finger numbness, and negative sickness psychology, should I get out into the world again?

Why? Well, because people are fun. They're the most fun you can have in life. Bad and good don't matter. Both are part of the package.

My old fears of people, public, and audience have disappeared. Thus, my entrance into the Performing Life journal. . . and more.

In regard to putting the "goals are fun" into practice: What's more important: Fun, or getting it right?

I think fun is the bottom line. Without it and the motivation it brings, you probably won't ever do it, never mind doing it right.

As an adult, it takes courage and daring to have fun. To know who I am and discover my authentic self, I will need to embrace the fun principle.

Kingdom of Fun

I've always wanted a calling, one similar to Moses'. I want to climb my own Mount Sinai and find my own commandments. Well, I've found them: my own personal orders, a personalized calling. And a great one it is!

It is to reclaim the Kingdom of Fun. In the process, re-establish enthusiasm, and restore the realm of joy and laughter.

Start with myself. Then move out to others. Start this morning with exercise meditation. Here's how: Focus on the feeling. Aim for a glow of pleasant vibrations flowing through my body, spreading to every corner and limb. Think and see this from the beginning, from my very first movement.

Drop any pressure to improve, finish, fill my numbers of reps. My goal for 2023 and beyond is to reclaim fun in everything I do.

CHAPTER TWO

Performing in the New Neighborhood

Wednesday, January 4, 2023
Introduction

Filling out all my folk tour registration orders is just plain *fun!* Seeing the sparkling constellation of tour registration grow before my eyes makes me feel joyous! Love is coming at me, thrown my way, from all directions! Exciting, thrilling. The feeling of being overwhelmed, resisting this celebration, is on its way down the drain.

Hebrew, and Languages

Is speaking another language joyful? The sound and vibrations feel so good. Am I avoiding the human pleasure of having a teacher? I'd gladly pay for its pleasure.

Remembering the Love, Joy, and Fun Motivation

The word "exercise" is so cold, mechanical, abstract, and joyless (like "medication" versus "medicine"). These words have no soul.

Yoga, running, dancing, weight-lifting have soul.

Take "exercise" off its fear base. (If I don't do it, I'll lose my flexibility and power, and be unable to work.)

Creating a "Novel"

Is my new journal a novel in disguise, with its own chapters, plot, and theme? I'd like to believe so.

Maybe I will try to expand it in this way. And perhaps, unbeknownst to me, I'm doing it already—creating a new form of "novel," my own.

The word "novel" means "new."

What else would I need? Nothing, as far as I can see.

I start my day with most of my important work already done. This way, everything after 9:00 a.m. feels free. I'd begin my day as if I'm on vacation.

Is there an exercise for vacations?

Yes! A light, pleasant, yoga Salute to the Sun.

Thursday, January 5, 2023
Celebration Day

Today is celebration day. I've moved from self-improvement to the calm connecting joy of acceptance. I had a great folk dance Wednesday evening, lively and wonderful, with new participants. And I'm celebrating my serious side as I now understand and accept it. My books work!

What's my initial response to success? Duality. On the one hand, my victory gives me a dramatic and beautiful shot of joy! But it lasts only a few minutes. Then comes the dramatic downturn with the suspicion that victory and success are endings, which, once celebrated, lead to "What now?" or "What's next?" In other words, I feel lost again. No end to searching, no end to pain.

So just as defeat is turned into victory, victory descends into defeat. Failure climbs to success; success dribbles into failure.

How to merge, connect, and defeat the devil of duality? How to move beyond this trap of success and failure, to synthesize victory with defeat?

The calm acceptance of who I am?

Monotheism claims the real self is connected to everyone and everything. It is beyond dualism, beyond success and failure, agony and ecstasy. It is the peaceable and beautiful land of Both and All.

"Just Do It" Anyway

Since today is a celebration day, how do I celebrate? Is there anything to do or not do? Should I just sit and vibrate? And how does "just do it" fit in?

Here's my idea: I will celebrate for a short time with some resounding Wahoos! But I can't let victory or defeat, success or failure, throw me off the path too long. Aim for a few hours, or even, as I get better at it, a few minutes. Let it out, let the ecstasy roll.

Friday, January 6, 2023
Duality

Short-term earthly goals are good. "Earthly" means, by definition, short-term. And this even if it is a lifetime goal. Create short-term goals along with awareness of the beyond- space-and-time infinite Higher Power.

Saturday, January 7, 2023
Most Important

We are all connected past, present, and future, forever. Having the power and confidence to believe this heals the divided mind and frees me from the fear of death.

Guitar Meditation Practice: Love Runs the World

Guitar playing is about love in all forms, on all levels—healing the universe, yours and mine. As I play guitar, think about (meditate on) this. Send each note to everyone and everything in the present world, past world, and future world. To All.

This is guitar meditation practice at its healing best. Heathy and redeeming. The All-In-One thought has high ranking and, some say, is the most important thought in the world.

Sunday, January 8, 2023
Stepping Out

The only way to escape from claustrophobia short-term is to step out of my body short-term.

The only way to escape from claustrophobia long-term is to step out of my body long-term.

Meditation: To step out of my body (box) and see the world from an out-of-body (box) point of view. As I play guitar, using my new step-out skills, step out off my instrument in the same manner. When I step out, what do I step into? The All.

Purpose of Classical Guitar: Metallic Intimacy with Zoom

The purpose of classical guitar is to bring inner peace. Calm. A meditation aid. To small groups. Intimate. It fosters connection and love.

A metallic, technical intimacy can be achieved through Zoom. Even through YouTube: a metallic, technical intimacy.

This is something I could do. The first spark of a possible idea.

Monday, January 9, 2023

Quite empty this morning. A pool of anxiety (directional energy) is building in me. I sense that everything will soon be dripping down the drain.

Say Hello, Then Wave Goodbye

Joe Freedman just sent me the Israel tour bill. I questioned it, think it's too high, and maybe a mistake. But am I right or wrong? So-called "realism" strikes—really, it's fear. Restrictions and limitations rear their ancient, hideous heads. A return of the sickening, fear-and-panic of having no money, financial penury, wiped out, a Bowery bum.

Should I flirt with this frightening, nauseating feeling? Or practice going past it to my post-Covid feelings of confidence and connection to All-Is-One?

Obviously, I need to choose the latter. And I will.

So practice life where I am now. Flirt with the old fears as one flirts with a passing cloud. Say hello, acknowledge their existence as former friends or, rather, acquaintances, then wave goodbye and move on.

Wednesday, January 11, 2023
The Post-Covid Life

If you practice something long enough, work on it, over time you do get better. You eventually succeed.

The historic Covid period has been my cleansing disease. My long-held attitudes were ripped out of me, washed away, and sucked down the drain. In this cleansed body and empty, purified brain, another attitude has flowered.

(Note: When writing this I suddenly felt the same pain in my left chest that I felt during folk dancing Monday night.

I sense it is a muscular pain, but worry: Could it be a heart attack? Or does this "pain," really a discomfort, reflect a "heartfelt" change in my attitude?

I sense it does.

Thursday, January 12, 2023
Floating

I have one goal: None. This morning, only habit and inertia are dragging me along. Floating in the clouds of a gray colorful pleasant uncertainty, I have no oomph or desire to do anything.

What do I want, or need? Maybe to float a bit more before I find them. Or they find me. *Doing nothing* may be the first step. Try it. See what happens.

Guides

Guides visit Earth in ageless forms. Although everywhere, they are often hard to recognize. But at least, in my folk dance travel business, I know my tour guides are heavenly guides in disguise.

Friday, January 13, 2023
Do The Minimum (But Do It)

I'm drained by the great Korean Netflix *Crash Landing on You* series, and the "heroism of stopping." Heroism? Yes. It takes courage. *Dare* to stop guitar, writing, and exercise. See where it leads. I'm only trading stocks now. That's it. I'm excited by it, but only by it. How long will this passion last? The skill of life is, after all, about riding the waves, not drowning under them. What about all my other interests and commitments? The answer: Tread water in them by doing the minimum. Yes, *the minimum*. Even if it is only five minutes—five minutes of guitar practice, writing, or exercise.

Saturday, January 14, 2023
Is Business An Art Form, or Am I Worthy?

Is business an art? Is organizing? Is my company, Jim Gold

International, a form of art? Are my skills worthy? Will my mother approve?

Growing up in our quasi-communist family, only art and intellect were considered worthy. Capitalists and business people were scorned. Artists and intellectuals were admired, respected, even worshiped as demi-gods. So my business, my company, would have to be an art to be worthy.

Well, it's not up to my mother. Only I can decide. Most of my life, I've been in conflict over this question. On the one hand, I love money and business; on the other, I love my art. Yet I've always been deeply involved with both. Constant paradox and conflict have ensued.

But now I'm at another turning point. I *want* to be worthy. In the process, I want to devote myself to miracles and the Divine. This means that, somehow, I want Jim Gold International to be in my personal pantheon of miracles.

Discouragement Versus the Life Force

I love stock trading. I'm proud and happy when I win and my stocks go up.

But I also hate stock trading. I'm discouraged and embarrassed when I lose, when my stocks go down. Losing makes me feel like giving up. And often I do. Yet after a brief period of "recovery," I always return to trading.

Why don't I give it up? Knowing how I've reacted in the past to personal and business defeats, I've discovered that somehow, deep within me, beyond discouragement, lives a "Never Give Up!" life force. It says "I'll die first. But I'll *never* give up."

I don't know where this inner strength comes from. It always appears when I hit bottom. I'm amazed by its sudden appearance.

The power of that *"never!"* saves me, pushes me back into the arena. So ultimately, although discouragement lurks in my neighborhood and sometimes knocks me off my game, it never wins.

Nice to know.

Sunday, January 15, 2023

Can I move from being a professional guitarist to being an amateur? From money-maker to lover? Of course, I love making money. But I also love love. The two can, needless to say, be combined in a strange, uncomfortable fashion. And I have done that for years.

My present money-making activities, otherwise called "business," are tours and folk dance teaching. They have become my "profession."

Now I'd like to become an amateur guitarist again—make playing a pure love affair.

Monday, January 16, 2023
The Gift of Sloppy and Imperfect

Stay sloppy and imperfect, and I can go at any pace, any speed. Accept sloppy and imperfect in the physical realm, and all guitar playing speed dreams can be realized.

Electric-shock finger therapy teaches me, creates this possibility, makes it so by reminding me that speed and mighty guitar playing are all in the mind. Paradoxically, sloppy and imperfect playing are the road to perfection.

Of course, in the spiritual realm there is no sloppy or imperfect, since there all is perfect. And of course, in the spiritual realm, there is here, and here is there. And since it is all one, physical blends with mental, and both fuse in the grand guitar spreading infinite joy throughout the universe.

But more of that later.

For now, I want to dive into light left-hand pressing. Recite the "Charge of the Light Press Brigade." Make Alfred Lord Tennyson proud.

Now I see (higher) purpose and plan behind my numb guitar fingers and the electric nerve shocks going through them. Light shocks me into pressing lighter in my left-hand guitar technique—to force me out of old guitar-playing habits, clear the fields, and make space.

The first result of such playing are dull, unclear, muffled notes. In the past, I would never have accepted such playing. But now I do. No doubt the impossibility of playing with numb fingers replete with nerve shocks has compelled me change my technique. I simply cannot press the strings without a shock. Very unpleasant. The only way I could play at all is by pressing very lightly. Well, what can you do? So I did it, and kept doing it, a little bit, day after day.

Tuesday, January 17, 2023
The Wisdom of Warming Up

I want my writing to be important. How do I know if it is? It's important if it helps others. How can I know if it will? First step: Does it help me? If it helps me, it will help them. Will the *Wisdom of Warming Up* help others?

I think so.

How did I discover this wisdom? It started this morning when I woke up afraid that, by diving into folk dancing, giving it my all, I would injure my body. But then, strangely, I felt glad to be afraid again. Why? My friend Mr. Fear was back as a motivator.

Then I asked myself: Is this realistic and true? Could I actually *hurt* myself by folk dancing too hard? Yes, my body hurts after folk dancing. But if I dance all out, give it my all, it doesn't hurt *that* much more than if I don't. These minor hurts are all part of the game.

So I reconsidered: Perhaps I'm restraining myself because something new is cooking inside. I'm holding back to protect this new idea, this new baby gestating, growing, and about to be born inside my mind.

Then I thought about the guitar. Yes, something new is happening there. Yesterday I found a new acceptance of sloppy, muffled guitar playing. This acceptance could fulfill my many-year dream of letting my fingers fly, of playing fast guitar through the infinite.

Yes, whether I'm folk dancing, playing guitar, running, weight lifting, even doing yoga, I'm afraid my old body will be hurt. But the truth is, in the past, my young body hurt, too. Things hurt whether you're young or old. So hurt is not really the issue. It's more about the *fear of immersion*.

And that's where warming up comes in.

I used to warm up all the time. Over the past few months, I almost stopped. Why? A macho thing. I wanted to prove I could appear before an audience and start playing guitar immediately. Full force. Simply dive in without warming up.

Why did I want to prove myself by doing such a stupid thing? Who knows? And at this point, who cares? And the fact is, it *is* dangerous to dive in without warming up. Warming up is for your protection. It's probably the only protection you can give yourself and have control over. It's an insurance policy against injury. And it works!

So I realized that, for dumb macho reasons, I had given up a good habit.

Wednesday, January 18, 2023

The specter of death is hanging over me this morning. If I can't figure out how to handle it, I won't be able to move on with life.

The pain of death and loss is just too great for me. On the other hand, I "know" that, as far as eternal truths are concerned, if I'm not in a fun-and-joy frame of mind, I'm off the mark and not dealing with loss and death "properly." I imagine there are sages who live eternity in the present. I'd love to be one of them. Unfortunately, I'm not. Death is still too scary, loss too frightening. Yes, I suffer from being human. What can I do?

Keep suffering is one answer.

Dive into the present is another. When I dive in, just do it, I forget about death, suffering, and loss. I simply skate along on the ice caps of daily activity. And I must admit that skating along can be, and often is, mucho fun.

So what is there to remember?

Eternity is in the present. Its daily medicine is to dive in. There's really not much else.

Either dive in and do it, or shut up.

So what is my next dive in, my next adventure?

Advertising: I'm becoming an ad man. The fun and joy of ads, using the canva.com site to help me design them, reaching out through email, my website, exploring, learning about, and adding social media posting in Facebook and Instagram to my repertoire.

Putting not only my tours ads, but also my local Monday night folk dancing announcements on my blog, posting them on Facebook, and even learning how to add Instagram, are part of this new ad-man direction. Remembering, and keeping it (note these action gerunds) in fun and joy, is the big challenge.

Revealing My Age

When Instagram asked to create my registration profile, it also asked for my age. I was amazed when I wrote it down. Really? That old? Should this creature still be alive? Shouldn't it have been in the grave long ago?

This is not a positive attitude. Is it healthy to see my age? Yes. It's a good reminder. But reminder of what? What are my age-viewing choices? I can either deny it or redefine it. So what does older age mean to me? Whatever I want, I think. And since it *is* my choice, I want to redefine its focus as healthy, good, proper, and *fun*.

Thursday, January 19, 2023
The Dive-In, Warm-Up Life: Another Post-Covid Gift

While practicing guitar this morning, I decided to forget about the right hand and focus solely on left, light-pressing guitar technique for a month. See what happens.

After that, I began my singing exercises. Then I somehow decided to combine my singing warm-ups with my Larry Bianco folk dance warm-ups.

The combo went like this:
- Six Breathers
- Six Screamers (three stomach, three index finger blows)
- Run in place alphabet vocals
- Vocalizing with Larry warm-ups

Then I picked up my guitar and started singing the Russian

beauty "Stenka Razin." My voice bellowed strong, loud, and clear. Great power and fun! It felt like the release of my true singing soul—another post-Covid gift.

Was it? Had I been avoiding my true singing soul for all my life? Today, somehow, I know it's ready for release from its long-time prison, ready to blossom forth from the depths of somewhere and charge center stage with power, conviction, and joy.

Friday, January 20, 2023
Fun in Advertising and Promoting Fun in Sales and Business

Business *is* my social life. Social life *is* my business! Quite a realization. This morning I woke up feeling good. I'm on track again. But on a different track. The biggie is: The best, and most enjoyable, way to promote my tours is to *call my clients!* Make it personal. I like my client travelers and dancers. Sure, calling them is more time consuming. But it's also more engaging for everybody, including me!

Imagine, having fun advertising and promoting my business. Totally new. A revolution in attitude.

Saturday, January 21, 2023
The Right Spot

Other worldly stuff: I almost dare not write about it. But I will.

I woke up this morning, read Hebrew with comprehension, and looked up "etymology," a Greek word for "truth, meaning," then decided to add Greek to my studies.

Etymology as history through the mouth, adventures of sound, music, tongue, and lang-uage.

By adding Greek along with etymology (*etymos* = truth + *logy* = speech), I'm also visiting with Greek gods, Nordic/Vikings gods,

Valhalla, and the Middle Ages, and 12th-century Nordic Sicily. I want to be in touch with the eternal places, and dwelling in history and etymology is one way to do it.

Then I started my guitar practice.

Playing Fernando Sor's "Etude No. 12," a feeling of joy came over me. Yes, that's what the piece expresses. A slight crack in the sky opened. I envisioned playing guitar beyond technique. As I laced and raced through the etude, I dove into joy and saw myself bringing it to an audience.

As I played the musette (bagpipe) measures of Bach's "Gavotte in D," I saw a destiny in my right-hand ring finger. New parts of my hand seemed to open up, calling for a new self-playing guitar with focus on emotions.

I pulled back to figure out what was happening. Was my future being dictated to me, sent down verbally through a Higher Power? Or was I creating another intellectual denial of mine?

Then I played "Alhambra," with total focus on thumb and bass. The right place to be. An eerie feeling of "creepy but beautiful" came over me.

Then I had a vision of Bernice and me sitting in a car "somewhere." We were looking at a wide-open, grassy field, peaceful and beautiful. "Alhambra" and thumb were sitting in the back seat, quiet and serene. It felt heavenly, all earthly problems resolved.

The right spot.

I pulled back a bit. Why was this scary *and* beautiful? It felt like death. Bernice and I were sitting in heaven, our earthly problems, symbolized by thumb and "Alhambra," all solved and meaningless. Earthly ties broken, but we were in heaven and together forever. Beautiful and peaceful, the right spot.

I started to cry for beauty and loss.

Sunday, January 22, 2023
Passing of the Body: A Practical Approach

Dare I be so rational about the passing of the body, about death, the "death thing"? Indeed, by calling it the "death thing," I am minimizing it, at least in my mind. How dare I? Part of me believes that, if I don't think about the passing, it will go way. Of course, I know that belief is false. Forgetting is the technique I use anyway.

But somehow this morning, after an eight-hour sleep, a rational vision has descended to my brain.

The passing of the body: a practical approach. What to do when swept away by the shock, chaos, panic, and sadness?

It's an organizational problem.

Will "dive in" and "just do it" work?

What other choice is there? Do I dare minimize the passing in such a manner? While my rational mind exists, I can still choose between the chaos and order, and answer a sad but daring *yes*. I'll cry on the side, in the middle, maybe always. But "dive in" and "just do it" seem the only way. (This is, I repeat, my rational, unemotional self speaking.)

Like planning and organizing a tour, or weekend or anything else in the physical world.

Earthly plans: physical and mental.

Spiritual plans: travel.

Rationalizing and minimizing this traumatic event: Perhaps it's a good way of looking at it. . .if it actually works for me.

How To Love Paying My Bills

Here's a good practice: Learn to *love paying my bills!* Start with my guide payment to Joe Freedman. How do I learn this?

Stop paying quickly, as I usually do. I do this so I "get *it* over with," "*it*" meaning the fear of giving up some of my security, namely, my money). Instead, before paying, think about *appreciating what he does, has done, or will do*. Then, gladly realizing his services, consider all the things he does to make me happy, gladly pay him.

Focus on Gladness

All this means learning how to slow down, not rush, not jump so quickly from one thing to another (monkey-mind), all so I can fulfill the dictatorial dictates of my self-imposed schedule.

Instead, better to focus on gladness: glad to play guitar, answer an email, pay a bill, on and on.

Quite a task! A difficult, constant, how-to-live-in-the-present challenge!

Reach for the Eternal

When I play guitar, I reach for the spiritual space, the eternal sound space beyond the physical and mental worlds. Where does the dissonant F sharp, the second note of the Bach "Gavotte in D," reside? What's the most joyous way to play "Alhambra"?

Aim for Timeless Gladness: The Fun Business Life

Check my tour email "interested" lists. Then *personally, email and call every interested tour client*. Pinpoint and focus my earthly efforts. Is that more fun? I think so.

Of course continue weekly group emails, advertising in all folk dance journals, and putting it all on my blog, and references my blog links in my emails.

Tuesday, January 24, 2023
Feeling Good

Work on the business and art (design) of the Bulgarian itinerary.

Great day of work yesterday. I was very busy. After three years, if feels like I'm suddenly back to work. And it feels good, even exciting. My brain and body haven't been stretched this way for years, since the pandemic started. During that period, lots of mental attitudes have changed, melted, molded, and are now in place. So I'm returning, not so much with a vengeance, as with passion and love.

I had a great workday yesterday, followed by another great night of folk dancing.

This morning I woke up on the border of feeling very good. I'm almost afraid to admit it. Things have come together. I'm in a good place.

True, I hesitate. I'm not used to waking up this way. I'm afraid all these good feelings will disappear.

And no doubt they will. Like clouds, all feelings come and go, appear and disappear, blow across my sky—high, visible, and beautiful—then move on, disappearing into the vacuum of the horizon.

So even though nothing lasts, why not take a chance and enjoy the day? Dive in. Grab the good feelings. Give myself a treat. Why not feel good. . .at least for one day?

Saturday, January 28, 2023
Nausea: Stepping into a New Identity

Interesting: I stepped into Hebrew directly, without any English translation, losing myself completely in the language, becoming a Hebrew-speaking Israeli. It made me nauseous.

Losing my linguistic identity, that is to say, made me sick. Apparently, this "identity" must be lost in order to master any language.

Guitar and Kabbalah

Imagine using my guitar for Kabbalah studies.

Performing in the old way is out, vanished, down the drain. Hebrew/Kabbalah/guitar/mysticism/secret/hidden are all scary, new, beautiful, embarrassing.

Why the latter? Embarrassment has "bar" in it, and the bar blocks the door. So embarrassment blocks (or signals) the flow and form of a kabbalistic guitar-playing power: secret, mystical, upcoming.

I'm reading two great books: Paul Johnson's *A History of the American People*, by Paul Johnson, and Franz Bardon's *The Key to the True Kabbalah*.

Sunday, January 29, 2023

The idea of guitar and kabbalah intrigues me. I wonder why. As for "Alhambra," maybe I can only play it with God's help. Certainly, years of practice have gotten me nowhere. No matter how many ways I try, nothing works. Maybe it's just time to give it all up and hand it over to God. Let Him handle it. I certainly can't. And not only for "Alhambra." Maybe for all my guitar playing. A prayer and beseeching.

Thus this intriguing connection between guitar and kabbalah.

Run Like The Wind

Friday I ran like the wind. First time in three Covid years. Yesterday I continued it and walked like the wind. Today, I'll try again: to run like the wind.

And note how good I feel! Running like the wind is the missing link. And this, of course, followed by a rest in the afternoon, and an evening yoga stretch session. Running and yoga stretches go together—and totally make my day! I feel like I'm back to normal or abnormal, whatever the case may be. And look how well and long I'm sleeping!

Wednesday, February 1, 2023
Folk Dance Artistry

I've never used the words "folk," "dance," and "artistry" in combination before. How did this happen? I woke up in the morning with a feeling of drainage. What to do about it? I had two choices: (a) Wait until it passes. Not good. Been there, done that. Also it "feels" bad. Or (be) dive in to my miracle schedule, no matter what. Sure, it also "feels" bad. But I *know* it's good. So do it anyway. That's what I'm doing. I start today.

I'm adding YouTube videos and folk dance artistry. What does that mean? Excellent dancing, plus excellent group dancing. Train my Monday night group for a YouTube video dance "performance." Folk dance artistry means my dancing has to be on a high level. But it means the same for my group! We're in it together. It means really teaching them so they'll perform well on the YouTube. We'll all improve together—going public is a big way.

I'll need a good body instrument for this path. I have to be in shape. Same for my group. Social director skills, leadership, organizational, and artistic skills, all combined into one.

This also gives exercise a new reason and purpose. Being in good shape becomes a performing prerequisite.

Guitar playing is slipping into the background. Where does it fit in? Truth is, given my present attitude, it doesn't.

What about Hebrew and language study? Well, at least there I'm *learning* something.

Without a new challenge or reason to practice guitar, why do it? In order to be inspired, to learn? I'll either have to find a new reason to play guitar or, like my teenage violin playing, it will fade away.

Thursday, February 2, 2023

I'm still recovering from the storm of joy, the shocking fact that, in January, all of my internal attitudinal changes during Covid, and all external tour and folk dance factors, came together.

Where is dissatisfaction now that I need it? I'm sure it will return; it always does. But for now, I'm in a quiet joy bubble. We'll see how long it lasts and where it goes.

The very fact I'm writing about it may mean it's coming to an end. Divine dissatisfaction will rise again, and I'll be on my way to somewhere else. It's the pepper in my food, the kind of irritation I like and seem to need.

The Fruits of Failure

Failure is good, especially when it peppers the soul. I need some failures to energize and spice up my day. Failure mean I'm aiming high. Where can I fail again?

Friday, February 3, 2023
Three Burdens Lifted

How to approach playing my guitar without carrying an "Alhambra" albatross?

(Reminder: The remnant of this formerly right-hand burden has for some time now been transferred to my left hand in the form of electric tickle, formerly numbness and shock in my fingers—a Sarnoian TMS transfer. Was my right-hand tremolo problem a form of TMS? It hurt mentally and emotionally, but not physically.

How to approach *business* without its similar albatross burden? Remember design, art, and the peace, beauty, and satisfaction of organizing.

Saturday, February 4, 2023
The Wisdom of "Just Do It"

I'm reading Hebrew very slowly. I'm not in a rush.

Why? I'm not going anywhere. I'm focusing on source and substance, sinking into the presence of each word.

Dare I think she will never leave me? That death cannot take her away? That we are and will be together forever? Dare I give myself such power over death? Is it really a choice? Yes. Of course, such transitions are events in the physical world. But attitude is always my choice. And I can choose joy and control over fear. I can *choose* to believe in the Eternal and its endless connection. If I do, it takes away all fear.

This is scary. The big question: Is death real or an illusion?

Beyond that, can I take it? Am I strong enough to believe life is Spirit?

Yes. But it's tough. And the big test, the real challenge of choosing between the two, comes every day.

I hate fear. But it is real and visceral.

I love Spirit. It is good, kind, and real in its own eternal way.

By embracing it, I gobbled up fear.

How can I learn to feel and know this in my core? Make it a practice. Practice thinking this way. If I do, how will I play guitar? My first thought is: It doesn't really matter whether I play or not. For that matter, beyond money, does it really matter if I do *anything* in this world?

In the physical world, it may.

But how much meaning does the physical world have anyway? Lots. Especially if you're in it.

Besides fear, though, the only real meaning is in Spirit. If that is true, then the only worthwhile thought is the grand connecting thought that, forever, All-Is-One.

And then connecting to all others is the only worthwhile thought to hold onto while I play guitar. It makes playing a worthwhile meditation practice.

So *that* will be my guitar.

Sunday, February 5, 2023
Money

I remember last year, as Covid ravaged my tour business, in anger and disgust over the small and often non-existent tour registration, I decided to raise my Israel tour prices by one thousand dollars. Fuck it, I said to myself, even if no one registers, I'll do it anyway. What's the difference *what* it costs if no one comes? It's just not worth running tours if the numbers are so small.

That was a year ago.

Now, strangely, suddenly, and miraculously, things have turned around. For the first time in my tour history, my Israel tour is full! I'm making a lot of money. Also, the fact that, when I lead, I am another expense, and I am *not* personally leading this one, is another saving. So, by *not* leading my tours, I am increasing profits! I'm so happy to see my worry that folks wouldn't register if I didn't personally lead my tours proved wrong.

Money equals security and power. It *is* the motivator that makes me work. And the more, the better! So yesterday I decided to raise all my 2023 tour prices, and folk dance class prices: Classes will now be $6.00 a leg, or $10.00 for two. And I'm accepting the folk dance booking in Teaneck's Temple Emeth that may soon be offered because, after days of indecision, I now have a *motivation*: I will make money!

Even selling my books now has a motivational source: to make money! Whenever I feel tired, lazy, unmotivated, depressed, just remember: by practicing guitar, or working on whatever I'm doing, from the skill I'm developing and increasing, I could soon be making money! When I told Bernice that money equals security and power, and, besides love, could be better than anything, she added that money also brings love, since she will love me more when I make money! So it's a win on all three levels.

While I am in this physical world, a love affair with money is healthy, good, profitable, and fun! How could I have missed this truth? Maybe I didn't, but its character was muddied by a desire for fame, acceptance, and success in competition with others.

I still want them a bit. However, wanting money is even better.

Of course, in the Big Long-Term Picture of Eternity, money is fluid, transitional, and temporary. But so is life.

The Lucky Disease

I suffer from the lucky disease: Actually, It's really not a disease, but a "condition," a dis-ease, created by time. But whatever you call it, it is still not easy. I'm not complaining, just noting and explaining. Any age has un-easy, dis-easy periods. No age likes dis-ease. So what's the big deal? Maybe there is none. With no let-up in sight, the only cure is attitude. This dis-ease can be handled, dealt with, even cured through gratefulness, the feeling that I'm lucky to have it.

Tuesday, February 7, 2023
Guitar

I need a reason to play, and playing for money is not enough. I need a better reason. Maybe just *play* is enough. Maybe to learn "just do it" is the new reason. I know playing guitar is good for me, but I don't know, or have forgotten, why. So "just shut up and do it" may be a good enough reason to play. And see where it leads.

I picked up the guitar after a two-week hiatus and started practicing, playing again.

And here's what happened: After a fifteen-minute traditional warm-up of legato, scales, and arpeggios, I played my usual Bach "Gavotte in D." Slow, focused, milking each note, Then the "others." (I don't even want to mention their names.) But again, I played them slowly, milking each note. And as I did, I just *knew* this way was *my* way, no ifs, ands, or buts. Audience, critics, onlookers, all forgotten, disappeared. I felt completely free. In fact, I had moved beyond even the feeling of freedom. I was just "there," just doing it.

Have arrived at a new place? It seems too good to be true. Yet it could be.

I'm at a new place everywhere else, so why not on the guitar as well? During the month of January, everything changed. Still, it feels so strange and different. I hope I'm right. But even as I hope, I *know* I am. I just have to get used to it.

Wednesday, February 8, 2023

February may be the month of low registration tour disappointment. Expect it. But continue the art and design fun business project, no matter what.

Dance Body

My dance body is the instrument through which beauty flows. Keep the instrument clean and sharp through the dance of yoga and flexibility, dance of running, and dance of weights. Add parallel feet. Focus on the outside leg, inside leg relaxed and loose. Redo my whole dance body, too. And my whole guitar body. How? What's new? It doesn't matter how I play. Why the discomforting nervousness this morning? I'm finished with my January happy and dynamic re-entry into the working world. But now it's February, and January foundations, now done and finished, have crumbled. I'm in a new month mentally and physically; I'm starting over from scratch, figuring out next directions, what exactly February will be all about. Again I am staring into the chasm of instability, wandering, wondering, and loss.

Thursday, February 9, 2023
Do Nothing Time

Admit it. I am in a bad place, despite my self-knowledge and wisdom. And what is this bad place? *No* place. Floating and directionless. Maybe "vacation" for two weeks is the answer.

It's do-nothing time. Tread water lightly.

Return to Guitar

Return to guitar with new meaning, vibrancy, love, and vengeance. Maybe February is a guitar month. The increased pain in my left folk dance ankle and knees is reminding me that I need to return to the center of my sustenance: my artistic roots. These were forgotten during my busy return-to-business month of January. I even gave up guitar for two weeks.

Time to nourish myself again, and drink from the fountain of beauty.

The mystery of "Alhambra." TMS panic that I won't get it.

Fast moving in calm, focused silence, the hardest thing for me. But it's the key.

I believe in optimism and progress.

Friday, February 10, 2023
Getting a Teacher

Getting a teacher means going public with my "hobbies." It means making them important. I'm depending on others for motivation and inspiration. Working with then, having expectations from them, motivates me through positive fear as my teachers become a new form of audience. And audiences used to strike terror in my heart. But I know how diving in, even into terror, is good for me.

Guitar

Arrogance and ego have kept me out of the bass. So much wanting to prove myself. But that has ended as guitar playing turns slowly into a "hobby."

Yes, a deep, arrogance hidden from the public haunts my being.

Arrogance is my form of fear, of hiding from others, protecting myself by feeling superior, separating from my love of them, and myself: fear of criticism, humiliation, diminishment.

That's the character weakness, the deficit that shows up in "Alhambra."

But no more, as "concert guitarist" evolves into an amateur, loving "hobby."

Where did this trauma come from? Does it even matter? Now arrogance has come out of the darkness, and, once exposed to the brilliant bass of "Alhambra" light, is slowly fading.

Thank you, Corona, for your gift of total destruction. During your first three years I lost everything. From this clean slate, I regrouped, and now, since January, I have returned with a happy vengeance.

Maybe you have to give up everything, lose everything, clear out all old self-definitions in order to find yourself.

Sunday, February 12, 2023

Why do I avoid Hebrew lessons, and have with Etty or any other Hebrew teacher, and this for years?

The negative is that I don't want to make my wonderful study of language another "important" self-improvement burden.

The positives are (a) having a teacher, or a trainer, motivates me; and (b) it turns my "hobbies" into something "more" important, makes them self-improvement goals, which again, motive me even more.

So why won't I dive into this obviously positive route?

Now I know. I don't want to "wake up," to be "bothered," by the burst of pre-performance nervous anxiety, that deep uncomfortable churning in my solar plexus, that is so deeply frightening.

I don't like to feel it.

Yet when I grab it, dive *into* my performance anxiety, accept the challenge, go through with the event, just do it, I also invariably learn something, improve, and become my own hero. In other words, I feel great!

Is this positive result worth the effort? No question it is. . .but that doesn't mean I'll make it.

But maybe I should. Since folk dance teaching is my job, I have to always show up and face my fear. Victory and some jubilation almost always follow. Thus the outside pressures of a job "force" me to make myself feel good.

No question creating another "outside" pressure by hiring a Hebrew teacher would do the same. But do I want to create such a challenge? Do I want to "bother?" Or would I rather rest, go at my own leisurely, unpushable pace, and sleep? I like sleep and rest. I also like motivation, having a destination, and following a dream. Is the dream of knowing Hebrew worth the big effort, "big" being defined as hiring a teacher? ("Hiring" because, for motivation purposes, I may need to pay for it. Or maybe not. Truth is, whether I pay or not, I'd still be nervous before each lesson. And maybe, evidently, I want to be. "Nervous" is my thing. Maybe it's a combination of having nerve, meaning courage, *and* "what a nerve!" meaning rebellion, boldness, standing up for what I want in the face of challenges.

I like that: It makes me proud to be nervous!

Monday, February 13, 2023
Appreciation

Appreciation and love are all I've got. Appreciate and love my wife, family, and friends. Appreciate and love all my work, skills, and talents; put them in the service of those I love, and all others. Damn the endings, but appreciate them, too. They belong to new beginnings, as well. Darkness belongs to the light, and light hides in the darkness.

Light is the All. As it illuminates, painful darkness lurks and slinks within its porous walls.

On Straightening My Feet

Straightening my feet is difficult and painful. My muscles ache and strain with the effort.

But the pain of effort is my life force moving forward, grabbing hope and power in the daughter of Life, aiming for the future while living in the present.

Beauty and Journal Writing

The beautiful poetry off and on in my journal: Send it to my Audience. Start with my family, friends, and folk dance family. (Dare I do this? This <u>is</u> new!) Show them who I am and, in the process, who they are.

Tuesday, February 14, 2023
Two Big Deals

The tours and their message are in place. The Christ phase of message and technical development is over. I'm now in phase two, the Saint Paul phase, spreading the gospel, the good news: advertising and promotion.

Also financially, I'm thinking of One Account. Bernice *or* Jim. This would mean giving up trading. Obviously, a good thing financially, mentally, emotionally, and actually in every way. Back to my Greenwich Village days of a bank savings account, small but satisfying, peaceful, secure, and stable.

These are two big directional deals.

I'm crying as I mourn the death of my stock market trading life. So many years, and now it's over. My forty-year rebellion is also over. How sad. . .but how healthy.

It happened so fast. I'm in shock. In three seconds the last leaf fell from the stock market day-trading tree. In one moment, a snap, and forty jam-packed years of trading action down the drain.

Wednesday, February 15, 2023

Bulgaria is a sleeper country. Even though few have heard about it, many want to go there in their dreams. It's off-beat, dreamy, and a bit wild. Its Slavic language puts pepper in your salt.

Folk dancers love it. They are the adventurers in this new land. The 7/6th ruchenitsas to 11/16th kopanitsas drive them wild. Once they hear the wailing wonder of the Bulgarian bagpipe, the gaida, they are finished. Immediately, think of Passover and Had Gadya, the goat of the gaida. Most countries have their own version of bagpipes, and they are pretty good. But nothing beats the gaida, especially when you've heard one hundred of them playing at once!

Why go to Bulgaria? For the wildness of the idea itself. Become your own Bogomil! (That's a member of a heretical medieval Balkan sect professing a modified form of Manichaeism). The term Bogomil in free translation means "dear to God" and is a compound of the Slavic words for "god" (Slavic: *bog) and "dear."

Then one day, through luck or circumstance they visit, and fall in love with its wild mountains, hidden lakes, and especially the people.

How to Feel Good

My walking with feet parallel has improved. Yet I woke up feeling so awful this morning. Is it worth dwelling on this misery? Acknowledging it? Yes. Evidently, feeling awful is part of me.

But I am the one who creates this feeling. Why do I do it? I must somehow want or need it. But *why*? Is it because I wake up every morning and forget my connection to everyone and everything? Yes. I don't feel good until I reconnect. Studying Hebrew, or anything for that matter, reconnects me. The attitude of "jump right in," "just do it," reconnects me immediately. And then I feel good. Simple.

Thursday, February 16, 2023
No Performance Anxiety

Free and floating again. I'm not satisfied; but I'm not dissatisfied, either. Last night's writing class helped, especially when discussing performance anxiety. It made me think about my own. I realized that, since the beginning of February, for the past two weeks, I've not been nervous before teaching my folk dance classes. This follows a first-time-ever, fun–in-business January. February started as a sales mop-up/semi-vacation month. I slipped back into a January tour-sales effort but soon realized I had completed that task.

And here I am free and floating in the middle of February, with no performance anxiety. I don't feel bad about this. I don't feel good, either. In fact, I don't feel *anything*. It's almost beside the point. And yet not feeling performance anxiety is a herculean achievement, a giant psychological leap.

Also, my desire for self-improvement has faded. I do think this is progress. And I have made progress too in walking with parallel feet. Even in guitar, my anxiety just dribbled away.

Get used to it, I say. Maybe, after so many years of stabbing myself with negative thoughts in order to motivate me, I've just gotten tired of them.

Friday, February 17, 2023

Since night and day exist, dark thoughts must be half of life, as are light ones. Why fight them? Better the accept the opposites into the Unity of Life. It's part of the struggle to stay connected, to know and remember One.

Go Deeper

I can always go deeper, deeper into the unknown places, the mysteries of the universe. What is the purpose of playing guitar? To explore the mysteries of the universe. It is a many-lifetime, infinite quest.

Saturday, February 18, 2023
Feeling Bad Is Good: Waiting Around For Love To Show Up

I'm getting sick and tired of waking up with negative thoughts. Is there any way to lose this habit? Probably not. It may be my nature. Can inertia, as a rest, be a positive force? Is there a way to make business and art "easy," or at least *do* them with ease? Do I have the energy and will power?

Maybe feeling bad about not doing things right is normal, correct, even good for me. After all, it is a good source of motivation.

Should I feel good about feeling bad, thankful and grateful for miseries?

On the other hand, I am "retired." This means I don't *have to* do anything. Why even want to be motivated? Is it an annoyance or a wonder? Or both? How about letting love be my motivation? Would that work? I could sit here leisurely waiting for the wind to blow love my way. That's the benefit of thinking "retired." I can luxuriate in letting love motivate me. No rush, pressure, or worry. And if love doesn't show up, so what? I can go to sleep, watch Netflix, or do nothing. (Could I even live like that?)

In January I re-entered the world of business, art, and work. I had so much fun doing it! But in February, I slipped back into selling them as an obligation.

Stop! Catch myself! My challenge is: How to love again?

CHAPTER THREE

The Moderate Life

Sunday, February 19, 2023

A wave of anger and energy powered by a touch of self-disgust means the cycle has turned, ended, and I know I'm back, my engine restarting, returning to the world.

I take these cycles personally, and I believe each moment within them is totally real and will last forever. And so I am trapped within them. But of course, no cycle ever lasts. And every "forever" belief I have disappears as the clouds of transient truths get blown away in daily reassessment. I'd like to have the wisdom to remember this.

But whether I do or not is beside the point. The cycle brings its truth, the clouds get blown away, a new day starts, and I soon accept it.

So what does today bring me? Connecting to my audience, equals love myself, equals All-Is-One. Self-improvement equals excitement.

Monday, February 20, 2023
Paths I Have Not Walked

One day at a time. I'm looking forward to today.

Writing my a.m. journal, I feel as if I'm taking dictation from something higher. Is this arrogance and hubris? Or simply true?

All is One, after all. Everyone has the power. But it must be accessed. I am somehow doing that. Dare I admit this? I used to say no; now it's *yes*. And I now live elsewhere. I want to be on paths I am not familiar with by my birthday, May 29.

Why wait? Why put it off? To let it gestate and flower, of course. But it happened today, now. One day at a time. *Carpe diem*. Waiting for my birthday to roll around is just another excuse disguised as wisdom. A too-familiar delay, a put-off tactic.

Tuesday, February 21, 2023
Going Out To Have Some Fun: Not Nervous

Last Wednesday night in writing class, the question of pre-performance anxiety we all discussed was very helpful, and I've thought about it all week.

Yesterday, on President's Day, the most amazing thing happened: I taught folk dancing, and I was not nervous. I had no pre-performance anxiety, no nothing. And all day long, instead of thinking about the show and mentally preparing, gearing up all my energy, instead I read Paul Johnson's *History of the American People*. And I did it an hour before leaving the house, focusing on it fully and freely, without a thought about my teaching performance.

In fact, I saw the upcoming folk dance class as a welcome break, a fun night out. I even got excited about it! All quite amazing. Suddenly, like the last leaf falling from an autumn tree, the idea of getting nervous before folk dance teaching just fell, became useless, and disappeared into the rump and rumble of dead leaves.

After teaching and another great night of dancing, I reflected on performance nervousness. I had considered it a forever thing, simply a part of my personality. But then I remembered back to a time before I got married when I was not nervous before a performance. In fact, before leaving for my year in France at nineteen, before conducting the Music and Art High School orchestra at sixteen, even before giving my prize-winning piano performance at thirteen, I was not nervous. Instead, I remember being excited!

So what happened? After marriage, suddenly, I had Responsibilities. I had to Take Care of a Family, make money, earn a living, be responsible, prove that I could be a true grown-up. In other words, prove that I could be a man. My child-like fun self, and even teenage and young adulthood with its wonderful innocence, were gone. And with their disappearance and my mounting responsibilities, coupled with the desire to be my own hero, take the chance and plunge of earning a living as an artist/entrepreneur, no matter what, the pressures came and along with them nervousness. I had (I told myself) little to no room to make mistakes, to fail. Each performance had to be a winner, so I could be recommended for the next job.

But starting this January, all the post-Covid inner cleansing benefits are coming my way, and I'm reaping their rewards. I'm suddenly enjoying my business, my art, and now, even performing without nervousness is in sight.

It's even beyond "too good to be true." It feels natural, obvious, a mere fact, not a big deal—an easy transition into the next kind of life. A return to the innocence of childhood, but now as an adult stepping into the freshness and wonder of the world.

I must say that even performing my World of Guitar assembly program show was once fun, especially when I did it for elementary schools and children. I never needed to prove myself as a guitarist, performer, or anything else. I could just be child-like, play, make wild jokes, and have fun. I felt very free before those kids. I could be my silly self, and they would laugh and love it with me.

Wednesday, February 22, 2023
Curiosity, Love, and Fun Are A Good Start

The nudge of curiosity and the rustle of the unknown rise unencumbered in the imagination. Losing interest in fear, anxiety energy dribbling away, draining into an ocean of boredom. . .is it true? Seems so. Accept it. Give up doubt. Ride with it, at least for today. Today performing fear seems silly. If my imagination has created this anxiety drama for so many years, what if it dissolves? What lies beyond?

Life itself is fun and games. Sometimes the games are deadly and painful. But they are games nonetheless. And imagination is the engine that rules the roost.

Where does this leave me? Lying on my back in the field of Awareness, staring into the wilderness with awe and wonder.

Perhaps I was never really nervous. Maybe it was just a game I played with my mind to make things interesting, to keep myself stimulated.

The classical guitar-impediment story, with its tremolo-and-speed stumbling blocks, may very well have been a fantasy I imagined into existence, a challenge created to keep me practicing.

Now that light has fallen across this dark game, will it still work? If I'm bored with fear, what will stimulate me now?

Curiosity, love, and fun are a good start.

Friday, February 24, 2023
The Down Side of Up: Joy, a Powerful Explosive—
Handle with Care

I slipped back into my old neighborhood and am there now. Legs, and fear of knee and thigh pain, are its expression.

Truth is, even though the political world outside that I read and hear about looks awful, on a personal level things are going very well. Business and art are moving smoothly and together. Mentally and attitudinally, I'm in a good place. So good, in fact, I can't take it! Imagine, having fun in my business, loving my art, and using it easily and joyfully in my business! Too good to be true—yet it is!

Perhaps I need this state of mind as a retreat, a vacation, to rest from the high-energy blessing I created, the shining, powerful (even overwhelming) light of finally becoming fun! Joy is a powerful stimulant and sometimes dangerous (so says Kabbalah), an explosive that must be handled with care.

Everything feels so good, I can't stand it! So I took a rest from it to float in the cesspool, drink some shit tea, and to recover some lost clay that slipped off building a fresh attitude in body, mind, and spirit.

The down side of up.

What to do? Nothing. Awareness is enough. Wallow in nutrient darkness a bit, appreciate the process, if possible, then roll on.

In Praise of Moderation

I always thought that, if you're happy, up-beat, and fun-filled, you're a winner; and if you're depressed, unhappy, and downbeat, you're a loser.

But joy can be stressful. So can its handmaiden fun. Maybe they are not healthy goals. Moderation, the golden means may be better. I used to tread the All-Or-Nothing road: the joy of victory comes with the agony of defeat; the glory of winning comes with the heartbreak of losing. Perhaps giving up these opposites in exchange for moderation would be wiser.

Aiming to walk this Road of Moderation is, however, a big shift for me. Did I just discover these values? I'd say yes. Dropping the extremes (which I used to admire and love!), and doing things in moderation, are their own art form.

Saturday, February 25, 2023
Fruits of Moderation

The thought of performing on guitar does not even enter my head! It's been a total cleansing! Now I can completely dive into the feeling. No outside impediments. What will it bring? So far, a powerful, outspoken index finger. It's fun to be so outspoken after years of hiding. My true tremolo self. Funny how moderation releases a powerful inner me.

Sunday, February 26, 2023
Aim for Accomplishments: The March Dictum

January was a burst-forth month, February one of retreat with focus on rest, vacation, and death. Now it's almost March. Rest and dreary images have run their course. It's up-and-at-'em time.

How did I get here? Thoughts about death are discouraging. And I don't like being discouraged. Why not live forever? Cycles, yes. Replacement parts and fixes, yes. Death, no. A rosy future creates a fairly rosy present.

Is discouragement a necessary reality? Or is it a choice? Better to choose cogitation, planning, thinking about what I want and will accomplish. Aim for that.

Monday, February 27, 2023

Folk dance is spirits floating in fun around the room, expressing themselves through bodies. Guitar playing is the same thing.

Woke up with zero ideas. Empty and spiritless. What to do? Keep doing, I think, the good things I know are good for me. Follow my miracle-schedule routine. Just do it until I remember why, until doing it reminds me of my purpose.

I must tank up with Spirit every morning. Without it, I am an empty vessel, a deflated balloon sitting flat on the earth. With it, I can conquer mountains, do anything, go anywhere.

What a strange and ephemeral thing is the spirit. Is it a passing cloud, or a permanent future? Intellectually, I know it is permanent. But emotionally, feeling-wise, it's the will-of-the-wisp, a cloud filled with pregnant waters, raining riches upon me. . .until it disappears.

Guitar

"Sor Etude 12." Light: the lighter, the faster and easier. Speed of light. Spirit is light in weight, and invisible, like sunlight. Heavy equals slow and strong. Light equals fast and *different.*

Seems I have to throw out everything learned in the past. I only built a solid, weighty base for the future, which is really light.

Tuesday, February 28, 2023
Renaissance

I've established my classic base, the Greek antiquity, miracle-schedule attitude, passed through the Dark Ages, with its cauldron of medieval Covid cleansing, and now enter a Renaissance moment.

Today is a mop-up day. Then what?

All feels the same. Why? I don't know, but I like it. I can't see changing any ritual, routine, or attitude. All are good.

And yet I feel I'm at a juncture, as if something is needed, a new energy source, but not necessarily a new direction. My "old" direction is adequate and good. So what to do—if anything?

I could return to the "same old" but *see* it differently. But isn't that the definition of renaissance? Does that idea in itself have enough energy? But there is nothing else I can think of. I like it all. I like my cycles. I am here and there. I have the right attitude and am in the right place, satisfied and somewhat arrived. With my classic period established, and medieval cleansing done, I have reached this place. It's neither sad nor happy, but a fact.

It has no surprise, no "Wow!" but a strange stable feeling instead, moderate and even.

It might make my pathway simply more enjoyable, without dramatic ups and downs. (This sounds a bit boring. . .but maybe not.)

Wednesday, March 1, 2023
A Renaissance Dream

Should I perform again? Could I? Is this a crazy idea or a reawakening of energy and fresh direction—wild and impractical, yes, but also possible, inspirational, and dynamic. The idea lifts me up.

Am I right to worry about age? Yes. But am I right to let it stop me, keep me from dreaming, blank out my vision, and hold me back? Is it better to drown in depression? To paraphrase Descartes, "I fight, therefore I am." The answer is: Go for the dream, no matter what!

Okay, so if I did, what form would it take? A one-man show. Guitar resurrected, but also singing—songs help me talk to the audience, and I need to talk to them, warm us up with vocals and ad libs. It's not about fame, fortune, acceptance, and approval, but about energizing *myself*.

Is the dream better, more necessary, than the reality? Inspiration lives in the dream. But once realized, the dream becomes boring.

Now, I am a dreamer, and my dreams never go away merely because the body tool of dreams changes. The dream creator remains the same, untouched by time, the engine-driving center of my spiritual life. During Covid, it was anaesthetized, put to sleep, driven into the darkness. Now, with the mist clearing, it is reemerging. Dreams are born in the imagination, which always creates new ones or reinvigorate old ones on a deeper level.

How could this apply to a one-man show?

Thursday, March 2, 2023
Making New Friends

"Love is all there is" sounds good. And it is good. But knowing this is also, somehow, a bit disappointing. Conquering fear used to be my great motivator. Most likely, it will still play a role, maybe a smaller one. I miss Mr. Fear and his electric charge. (But just a *bit*.)

What about my old friend Larry Depression? With love now ruling the roost, there's not much room left for him either.

In this strange world, I miss my old friends.

Well, maybe it's time to find new ones.

I can start by meeting Mr. Hebrew. Hocham is his first name. I also want to meet Mrs. Guitar. Or is it Ms.?

Does personalizing these archetypical friends mean I'm passing into humor? Maybe.

Michelle or Larry Guitar. Or Mr. and Mrs. Herma Phrodite? Perhaps a gathering of former friends is in order. Maybe they were always friends, only now they look different. Or rather, I see qualities in them I didn't before. Maybe it's time to reconnect with them but in a different way.

No more separation between then and now.

Evidently, I always had one friend, angel, and guide. Only I didn't know it. But now I do.

The battle is over.

As for guitar playing, I may have to slow down for awhile to sandwich some love in between my thumb and fingers.

Friday, March 3, 2023

Guitar: A new approach: Eliminate the whole tremolo! (Play as if no tremolo.) Only thumb and bass. Yes, it's a trick of mind and music. But it could work. Try it for awhile. See what happens.

Acceptance of rest and "doing less" as a health and training pillar. It goes with *March as Moderation Month*. I used to be a radical, go for high, wild, and crazy passions; I idolized extremes and the highs and lows, and the pains and pleasures that came with them. But something has changed. Moderation, and the idea of rest, are appearing on the horizon and moving swiftly across the sky, eradicating the wild light with its extremes of heat and cold, and, in the process, creating a fresh sun.

Is there a sun of moderation? Must be, because I'm beginning to see one. It could be a stage, or that I'm getting smart, part of an attitude coupled with a coming life.

This moderate self includes all extremes past and present, rejects nothing of the old, incorporates all: calm and collected, the peaceful island after the stormy ocean voyage.

Health and Work

It's healthy to work hard, and it's very healthy to work very hard. In fact, it's exhilarating.

Saturday, March 4, 2023
An Important Truth: Going for the Useless Will Make Your Day

An important truth: Uselessness can be useful. How does this work? How do you move from useless pleasure to utility, from "I like it as a good-in-itself" to "How can I use it practically in real life to help myself?"

I am asking a moral question: Is the useless good or bad? Descending, although necessary, is bad. (That's why it's called "down.") Ascending is good: Staying up there, high and floating, the longer the better, is nice. The higher you go, the better it gets. (That's why it's called "up.")

Best is aiming for what's good-in-itself.

So although my pleasure in learning and knowing the roots of Hebrew words is basically useless, it is still fascinating and fun, which is good for spirit and inspiration. Filling the spirit with inspiration creates an engine that motivates the lower self—and practical action is the result. So the useless can indeed be useful.

Sunday, March 5, 2023
Striding the (Fun and Useless) Yes Path: Fun in the Cauldron

March is the marching month, the go-get-'em month. February's rest and vacation are over. Back to exercise, pain, and struggle. I have learned that you need to choose between growth and comfort. You can't have both. I choose growth: hard work for the rest of my life.

We had lunch with my sister and Ellen Gilbert. She talked about studying Italian using the Babble program. I told her about my language studying conflicts. Very cleansing and illuminating for me.

Result: My basic love is of sound and its music. Articulating the sounds, holding them in my mouth, swirling them around with my tongue, are so much fun, give me such sensual pleasure. It's the fun of speaking a foreign language. A good-in-itself, useless and wonderful. Have I been denying myself this privilege and pleasure?

Same with singing and its vocal, throaty, emotional, sensual pleasure. Another good-in-itself.

Have I also been denying myself the former pleasures of my body? This started, I believe, with Covid and finished with stents, which stopped my running and inhibited the physical pleasure. Fear replaced giving it my all, whatever "it" was. I used to get so much pleasure in yoga stretches, running, feeling the wind and air caress my body, even the thrill of lifting weights in the gym. I slowly gave up all these goods-in-themselves pleasures, and in the vacuum that followed, fears of health and death flowed in. These wonderful practices became "useful" in the sense that they were used, not for fun and pleasure, but for the purpose of *making me healthier.* Ugh. Using something for an ultimate purpose may get you there, but it is no route to happiness. And if you do get there, you wonder why you bothered in the first place. Without good-in-itself personal pleasure, without love, joy, and fun in the *process*, everything dribbles away.

I used to have it, but I lost it. Time to go forward by going backward. Returning to voice and body pleasures is a gigantic leap into a different direction, striding on the *yes* path.

It boils down to a question of courage and attitude. Sure, pain and pleasure mingle—and can hurt. But growth and comfort are incomputable. Is it fun to be boiled alive? Maybe.

Get Back to the Sensual Life

Guitar contains the sensuality of the fingers. I need to get back to the sensual life. It nails me to the present and give me a good reason, a good-in-itself, fun, to return to concerts—if I ever get that far.

Fast

Fast is another pressure. Maybe I don't even have to go fast. No fast guitar, fast running, fast dancing, fast anything. I don't mind *going* fast. In fact, it's fun. It's the *pressure* to go fast that I want to give up.

Bring Back the Gaida!

I am playing my gaida after a long and fruitful slumber; and today I collected three key elements of what I want: language (voice), singing (voice), and gaida (breath, Bulgaria, off-beat, show business, sound). So I am treading the Gaida Pathway with its off-beat sidekick Bulgaria, which opens the Humor Passage.

Monday, March 6, 2023
The Magic Providence Spot

The Magic Providence Spot exists forever, and thus cannot be developed or improved. It can be first discovered in body parts like the index fingers and knee. But once it has been, it can be expanded to include the whole body, the whole world.

Tuesday, March 7, 2023
Memory

Yesterday I knew what was right. I had it all together. I began this morning by totally forgetting it. Indeed, each day starts afresh, and this through the power of forgetting. Did I forget them because I have a bad memory? Or was it because yesterday's learning has been absorbed, its lessons now in my bones and blood, and I'm ready to move on?

Guitar and Dance

The magic spot exists for guitar. It's easy. My tremolo and arpeggio fingers have gotten faster and stronger. Multiple repetitions make it work. This is good.

Body Works

Maybe it's not age but training and life style. I hate to admit it, but, truth is, since Covid, my life style has changed. In the process, my body has become weaker. What happened?

Before Covid:
1. I taught two two-hour dancing classes a week.
    a. Plus a two-hour Darien class once a month.
    b. After classes I warmed down with an hour of yoga.
2. I ran.
3. I trained with Rick twice a week at the gym.

After Covid:
1. I dance two times a week—one one-hour class, one hour-and-a-half class.
    a. Stopped yoga warm-downs.
2. Stopped running.

3. Rick once a week
4. Stopped leading tours
    a. I do lots of desk work and sitting.

No wonder I'm out of shape and my body hurts. It's March. Business and art are all in order. Only "exercise" (I hate that word!) is left. It's obvious what I have to do, only I'm not ready to think about it yet.

Wednesday, March 8, 2023

Discouragement, or Inspiration and Curiosity: It's My Choice
Will I be discouraged or inspired by stumbling through Hebrew this morning? It is my choice.

I could *choose* to be inspired and curious, instead of discouraged, when I encounter stumbling blocks, slow progress, and other problems.

With regard to playing guitar, I just crossed over from inspiration and curiosity to the desire to *improve*. Is that good, bad, or different? It certainly a different feel. Inspiration and curiosity feel calm, reflective, and peacefully distant. The desire to improve is more frantic, angry, and self-involved—a different earthy, aggressive energy.

Thursday, March 9, 2023
Sales

I like the process of selling things. It's fun, and it doesn't matter what I sell. It deals directly with people, and I like people. Results that may come in are an extra blessing.

Had two teeth pulled and implants put in. Hurts mucho. What is the positive symbol of new teeth? A better, stronger bite!

I'm implanting a stronger, tougher, stand-up-for-yourself character in my teeth. Does this mean tougher knees and fingers? Could be.

What does arthritis of the personality really mean? A stiffening of the mind often reflected in the body. But a tougher self has the dental power to bite into the opposition, and, with tougher knees, stand up for its rights! Sure, it hurts. But so what? That's the price of growth.

Creating Strong Teeth

Where does Kabbalah fit in? What is the symbolic meaning of this process, the purpose and power of creating strong teeth?

I want and need to make this painful process worthy and meaningful. I need and want more *bite* in my life.

Sure I'm imagining this, making it up, creating, choosing to interpret the symbols of my own dental process. Does that mean it is right, wrong, or irrelevant? Only I can know the answer. There's no one else around. So I'll decide: Yes. Strong teeth mean implanting fresh confidence, meaning, and power in my self.

Writing and Strong Teeth

Reading my Barry-edited work on the computer is the "throw-away" approach, coupled and tinged with self-diminishment. Printing them, and then being able to go over each word slowly, means I'm making them important. And from there, it means *doing* something with them! It would no longer be "throw-away" stuff. Promoting, publicizing, advertising, announcing—whatever. I could add folk dance and even guitar videos to this. Indeed, I would be making me and what I say more important. (I rebel, resist, hate, and fear it. But that's where I am.) I could even start putting stuff on Facebook with no consequences. Writing, folk dances, even guitar: All move together as one self.

The Habit of Self-Diminishment

My habit has been to deny the good stuff I've done or written. I want and try to forget it as soon as possible, dismiss its (my?) importance, and "move ahead." Perhaps I am coming to the end of this dilemma. Love of others can't grow until love of self is implanted.

Two contrary streams meet in stalemate.
1. I don't believe in the progress I am making.
2. But I *am making* it!

A stalemate can't last. One side will win. And I *know* it will be the "I am making it!" side! I'm playing with hesitation, making a game out of stalemate. But since I know the winner, why not simply accept him now? After all, March *is* the marching-forward month. It's reasonable that "Alhambra" and the Sor "Etude No. 12" are flying.

Saturday, March 11, 2023
Discouragement Versus Hope

Discouragement tells me I will always remain the same; no matter how much effort I put in, nothing will ever change. Why bother trying? Discouragement makes me soggy and sad, a morass of solitary confinement, stuck in a dump of mud. Hope is my silent motivator. It pushes me into the nonexistent future where the possibility of improvement lies. It's so uplifting. It makes my spirit soar. I want to sing and dance. Hope brings pleasure and happiness to my soul, and thus to other souls as well.

I prefer hope to discouragement. Yet I am stuck with both. Can something be done about this dichotomy? Or is a split mental state a normal environment for the competitive mind, a form of psychological entrepreneurship, a capitalism of the brain? Maybe I should adopt a *laissez faire* attitude toward my mind and let these forces (hope and discouragement) fight it out unencumbered. No conscious mental or government interference. What would Adam Smith say? Or is such a split (schizophrenia) the natural state of man?

Hope is a blind force but positive in nature. It does not see the future, predict it, but says there is one, and its results could (with effort) be positive. As an agent of life, it energizes the mind, propels it forward.

Discouragement negates energy; smothering initiative, damming up incentive, it siphons off the power flow into a desert wasteland. It is the brake of rest and inertia. Sometimes disguised as safety, it kills exploration. As such it is an agent of death. Yet just as life and death go together (in the material world) so (it seems) do hope and discouragement. Or is it just me?

How To Be a CEO

I always like the idea of a career I haven't tried. Is it now to be CEO of my company? Seems so. Evidently, I'm in the adman and salesman phase of my life. This has always been part of my *business* life, but now it is more. At this point, I no longer have to create more products (although I will because creating them is my nature). Blossoming now is how to sell what I've got—the opening even embracing the salesman self.

I have three product lines:
1. Jim Gold Tours (main business)
2. Jim Gold folk dances and dancing (side business).

3. Jim Gold books (side business).

So far tours and folk dancing have been and remain viable businesses. Books remain in the background.

Will I put in the energy and effort into book sales? An old question and story. Only now, I don't have the ego problem I used to. These books were written by Jim Gold, not me. They belong to him. It's easier to sell other people than myself. So since he is no longer me, it's easier to sell his books. Distance in time has helped diminish this ego problem, while the idea of dying, and death itself, have made it disappear almost entirely. So on to a multi-faceted career!

Most of my focus and energies in coming days will be on being the CEO of my JGI tour company, which, at least in number of tours, is expanding rapidly. How to organize, run, and sell these will be my big challenge.

March Leap

It means that writing, guitar playing, and even folk dance teaching, are sinking into the "hobby" section. There they will join study: language history study, and perhaps even exercise (running, gym, and yoga)—all side interests formerly of miracle schedule fame. (Why do I say "formerly"? I'm not sure. Something changing on the horizon.

CEO, though, is now my main effort. How to build my company. Should I hire people? And how do I do it?

Starting Fresh

This implant knocked pain, and "sickness" knocked everything I am and was doing, out of the picture, cleared the deck, cleaned the slate. Everything I used to do is either done or not important anymore.

Monday, March 13, 2023
Aiming for Dental Freedom

All I can think about today is healing my tooth. It is consuming my mind, which there is nothing like pain to focus.

And psychological pain feels like a *luxury* next to the physical variety.

Maybe the purpose of guitar playing is not to perform for others but to heal the self! Maybe I focus on the audience because it is too painful to focus on me.

Can guitar playing help teeth, even heal mine? Can the beauty of music distill it, cause it to drip-drop away? Is playing my medicine?

Seeing classical guitar as a healing modality is a totally different orientation for me. It means traveling inward, visiting the lonely self stranded in space, staring into the vacuum searching for a savior. What is a lonely tooth lost in space to do? At this point, probably waiting it out is the answer. I'm ready for *mouth* return.

Tuesday, March 14, 2023

The sage Walawoosa came down from the mountain. He surveyed the crowd gathering before him, stepped to the microphone, and said, "Man is born sick and lives to be cured. Man is born tired and lives to rest.

Man is born with a limp and lives to walk straight. Man is born bad and lives to get better."

Thursday, March 16, 2023
"The Virtue of Your Work"

"Believe in the virtue of your work," Barry said. Believe in yourself and your creations. Of course, I like it. I'm diving in. Last night, with "virtue of my work" in mind, I edited my *Performing Journal*, starting from the beginning. This morning it's the virtue of "Alhambra." I rediscovered the accented second and third beat as most important. The virtue of my playing: Practice the "I've got it" feeling. Does this go with Dr. Weisman's steam-shovel dig into my gums, and the new and better bite it will eventually create? Make the pain worth it. *Turn orthodontic misery into victory.* Let my screaming implants help create a powerful dental "Alhambra" with more bite than ever! Yes, grab it!

The Last Leaf Fell from the Tree

I have sold all my trading stocks. The last leaf. This is a big deal. I gave up my last put-down place, my last blockage. Yet dropping it felt easy and right.

Will this lead to virtue in guitar playing? This mainly through "Alhambra," queen of mental blocks, with monumental blockage, and writing, also a virtue and doubt-blocked (am I good enough?) for so long. I sense it will. I wonder what eliminating this long-term poison will do for and to me.

Motivation and Hope Are Forever

My teeth hurt. I suffer in many other ways as well. In fact, suffering governs much of my life. "I suffer, therefore I am, was, and will be." It hurts to suffer. But I endure it anyway. Does anything good come from it? Endurance comes. Endurance is good. After you get through a bout of pain, you know you're tough, strong, and resilient. You'll survive when the going gets rough. (Nice to know.)

So suffering develops the inner strength, toughness of direction, perseverance, and principles of dignity and survival that we call *character*. What about improvement? I like to improve. It's my source of motivation. My desire to improve is based on the hope that, through practice, study, or whatever, I will get better. Thus, the benefits of suffering: If it produces endurance, and endurance produces character, then character can create hope. And hope is my source of motivation. St. Paul said he rejoiced in his suffering! I'm presently in the St. Paul stage of my life, spreading my gospel, the good news about folk dancing, folk dance tours, my books, and guitar playing. So rather than feel badly or, even, ashamed of my suffering, I need to be proud of it, to embrace the pain. Not only does it make me my own hero, it fills my sails with forward energy, creating billows of hope for the future. Through my struggles, challenges, pain, and practice, I can ride the motivation horse into the future. . .and improve! And alive or dead doesn't matter. (Although it's nice to appreciate things as they go by, they are really beside the point, because the future marches on whether I'm here or not. Future is forever; so is the past. Co-existing (here-and-now) in the present, they live in my teeth, in the words I just wrote, and in the guitar notes I will play as soon as I finish writing.

Friday, March 17, 2023
Touching the Land of Virtue

Virtue gives me the strong bite I wanted. Symbolically, it connects the (im)planting of writing and guitar virtue to the dental implants that are presently creating such pain in my jaw. Of course, there is pain in uprooting former ways of thinking, and glory in the (im)planting current ideas.

You must dig a hole before you plant a seed. *Symbolically*, it all fits together. How about in *reality?* I think it fits together there, too. Symbol and reality meet, collide, clash, crash, make adjustments, and eventually merge into one. So here's a birth of virtue . . .yet I am wrathful, furious. How strange.

I took a walk and my legs were stretched and flying, offering a revived sense in my stride of power, stretch, and tingle.

Virtue on three possible fronts. All good stuff. So why, after a two-hour, late afternoon sleep, did I wake up so furious?

Am I angry because I lost my put-down cover? It just fell off, revealing an exposed, raw center of power: wild, wooly, unstoppable, and free. The controls are off. Only annoyances reign. I'm naked and open.

Perfection Versus Fun

I'd love to be perfect and divine. Yet divine and sloppy may be the best I can do. I roll between perfection and fun. Does virtue has a place here? Is it fulfilling to be perfect? Does *aiming* for the summit bring satisfaction? And what's perfection? Is reaching for an unattainable goal fulfilling? Or does happiness reside in accepting limitations. And wisdom means living in the wriggly borders of divine sloppiness.

Can't Beat a Shining Sun!

Divine sloppiness is the human road, the best one for me. Aiming to get better is good. But aiming for perfection is inhibiting.

Unrealistic pressure only gets in the way of dreams by creating dark days, waking nightmares, and dissatisfaction. Joy, by contrast, clears the clouds, makes endorphins flow. You begin to shine.

Monday, March 20, 2023
Sales Meaning

I'm at the cusp of a great internal discovery on the guitar. I wonder what that means.

Descending to the bottom of the personal, I lie on my foundation. The guitar will express my person. But what is it?

a. A renaissance person. All studies.
b. A unique, standing-with-others person, but alone. (Perhaps leading.)

It's one day to spring, a good time to start. My artistic purpose feeds my business purpose. Sure this analysis is imaginary and poetic. But it could also be true! Only I can decide.

Imagination creates the power of self-belief, based on virtue. Can I hang on to this "fantasy"? It is such a seriously good one! Paradoxically, the larger meaning of "personal" is *universal*. One is *everyone*, alone is *with others*, *unique* is universal, all are one. How strange is this alone-and-together world!

Person comes from "*mask,* false face" in Latin. The mask of ego blocks the universal meaning of the person-al.

All this shows why I *have to* give a concert, either alone in my living room, fed by audience vibrations in my imagination, or for real people in a public setting. Either one is okay. But the thoughts must be others-and-I. Con-cert is the one-ly Truth. That's why the idea keeps haunting and pursuing me. Playing alone is merely a practice and preparation for others to join. (That's why I love the group dancing in my folk dance classes).

Same with writing, fiction, and my stories. Sales is the effort of connection. Connection heals. No connection hurts. Sales rejection, alas, also hurts. When others fail to affirm you, it pains the soul.

But art and business can combine. When they do, they create *sales meaning*—a vibration, a joyful connection, beyond the commercial and aesthetic.

Blast of Joy

I'm stunned by the actual wisdom of what I've just written. I need time to recover from this virtue in action. Truth is, I always need time to recover after I write. Perhaps the release of it is such a powerful stimulant (maybe too powerful) that I need a rest when I'm done. It can and does knock me out.

Or maybe I just can't stand the virtue of my skills, along with the wonder of exercising such a gift staring me in the face.

Laughter or Tears

Maybe up and down will always be my lot. I'm a tortured soul. That's just the way it is. And what after all, as an artist, can I expect? But if that's the case and lots of downs are part of it, what about the ups? I'd like a few of them, too. Would consciously writing my humorous, off-beat, wild, and crazy stuff help? Would it save and cure me? There's no cure for up and down, but might such writing be a good way of consciously handling them?

Can I purposefully work to save myself pain and suffering? Or do I *like* pain and suffering? Although it hurts, it also makes me laugh: the *ironies* of suffering, its paradoxes and contradictions, the wild fantasies of up and down. Sure it hurts. But it's also good for laughs. Do I want to give them up just to avoid pain? Could I even if I wanted to? Strangely, I think not.

It's probably better to use my pain, turn it into something funny or sad. Creating something, anything, may be the only answer to suffering—a way of handling the vicissitudes of life, since there's no way to get rid of them.

How quickly the vacuum of stock market trading got filled. The pain is almost gone, along with the memory. (We'll see how long this lasts! Am I tempting fate, and the strength of my determination with this last sentence? Maybe. But I'm still at a crossroads place, maybe for the reset of my life!)

I have somehow added talking, going public with etymology love. And talking about it seems to be working. People are interested, to my surprise and happy amazement.

But my main learning about where I presently am is through Hebrew. My reading and study are slowing down into the quantity and quantity of each word! It feels like I'm falling, and sliding further, into depth, and in the process, moving further into quality and depth.

Guitar Practice Reward

What is my guitar practice reward? To play some pieces as *fast, sloppy, and with as much fun as I can*! These include Bach's "Bourree in B minor," and "Gavotte en Rondeau," and flamencan pieces.

Well, if that is my reward, why not take it now? Think about that! Could my new March-ing orders include taking my rewards *now?* Imagine, *rewarding myself now!* An amazing and wonderful leap into the hugging arms and kisses of in-place direction.

Tuesday, March 21, 2023

I feel as if I have had a double surgical removal. Fear and pain have fled. I expect the pain to return. But fear? As a motivator? This former energy source has somehow been excised. For a while, the ensuing vacuum was filled with tooth pain. Now the pain has subsided, leaving another vacuum—but the old fear has not rushed in. No, no. I remain empty, and the energy, once based on this fear, has also drained away.

Space for a different view of energy: I'm on the cusp of an altered source of motivation. The up-and-down, ever-fluctuating high/low of trading stocks no longer serves.

So I'm standing at the door of Puzzle Land.

Calm Duty

I think the answer is to calmly follow my path and do what I do. The golden mean hits the old Wild West town.

As Andrew Carnegie said, first get rich; then it is your duty to give it all back. Money is good. Wealth creation is the first step. But money is not the only wealth. Riches in experience, talents, and skill work, too.

Guitar: Show and Share

A bit of "Leyenda" and "Soleares." Then a loose blast of fast, sloppy, and fun "Gavotte en Rondeau." Yes, that's it! And even a bit less sloppy in the fun!

The word "sloppy" sounds negative. But perhaps I need it during this transition. And here's a truth: When you play fast-and-fun, it's not even that sloppy! And so-called sloppy slowly fades into fast-and-fun, and soon becomes just fun!

Fun equals joy. Joy is the ultimate giving. Fun is the pinnacle. Upon arrival, what a gift to show and share the view with others!

Thursday, March 23, 2023
Meaning Versus Leisure and Safety

Without meaning and purpose, life is meaningless and purposeless. Because of the extreme wealth of our society and the ease of daily existence, with all its make-things-easier devices, folks have slowly embraced leisure and safety over meaning.

Ever Yearning

I will never play good enough; I will never *be* good enough. And maybe that's the way it is supposed to be—ever reaching for the stars, never arriving except for brief moments of ecstasy.

That's why, for mankind, pain and suffering (even though they are a choice) cannot be avoided. In this earthly existence, they are forever. Perhaps it is our task to realize they are part of the show, and if possible, through humor or other means, to make them part of the fun. Can they be, *must* they be "fun?" Well, why not?

Evidently, frustration, pain, and a choice of suffering are the human lot. Or at least my lot. Are these constant struggles worth a good laugh? Probably. Am I diminishing their importance by laughing at them? Probably. Are they even important? Yes, of course...but only *in the moment*. Beyond that, although they constantly reappear, probably not.

Okay, time for me to have some cookies and ice cream. . .and move on.

Sunday, March 26, 2023
Deep Musical Study

I need to reread musical theory and the nature of notes, delve further, deeper and wider, into the next music path for me to follow. It's not about guitar anymore, but rather about the nature of music in general. The guitar just happens to be the instrument of learning and expression that I choose to use. Could be voice, too.

Diving into the Maelstrom, Riding the Whirlwind

However, after an hour of this long, deep study, I still have to let myself break loose, go wild, drop the trimmings, and dive into a maelstrom, ride the whirlwind of unleashed musical fun! Should doing that be part of each practice session? *Yes.*

An unleashed "Alhambra" and "Leyenda" a day

Keep the doctor away.

(Throw in a few flamencan dances as well.)

Exercise between guitar practice rounds. Use light yoga stretches and routines to calm and engage the body. If the body is not calmed, its twitching and energy breakouts distract the mind. Exercise calms the body and thus frees the mind to focus clearly.

Thus, guitar practice and exercise, yoga stretches, and so on are connected. Add some vocal warm-ups, too.

Monday, March 27, 2023

Etymology is my form of history. *Horizon* comes from Greek "horo," circle, limited circle.

Aorist: *not* horizon, limited, indefinite.
Aphorism: cut off, short, pithy

The Performance Life Is Me

Am I passing out of, beyond, the *Performance Leaf?* Has it become part of me? Mostly. I'd say yes. What's the next leaf, then? There's always more.

Guitar:

Let loose "before my time." Opening up on Sor's "Etude No. 12." After twenty minutes I'm loose and ready to go. I'm playing it fast-as-hell, wild-in-the-whirlwind, at a dizzy-and-beyond pace. I'm going so fast I don't know where I am anymore. See where it goes.

What happens when you go beyond the speed of light? What happens to the horizon? Does plunging into the unknown help others? I'd say it does, paradoxically, by going beyond. Only, since you are dealing with the unknown, you don't know how.

Thursday, March 30, 2023

Why this deadness, this retreat of enthusiasm? Fear of being hurt, that's why. It started with dental pain and has lasted until today—my worst ten days of pain in years (maybe even ever).

No doubt it was a smart energy retreat to fight for body survival. My body knows how to take care of itself. It also no doubt knows how to re-ignite enthusiasm.

Interesting to note: Although my teeth screamed with pain, I did not *suffer*. Pain cannot be avoided, but suffering's a choice. So even when I was screaming, I did not suffer from cosmic depression. Energy went into healing the body, which it eventually did. Now I can feel the first-time ripples of enthusiasm "rising from the dead." I'm sure they'll soon be waves again.

Will I enter these notes in my journal? Probably not. I'm just so sick of this transition process! I have been through a big trauma. First, three years of Covid. Then ten days of tooth extracting and implant pain. Time to feel sorry for myself! Some good old self-mourning is in order. Will self-disgust follow? Probably. So will I write about all this in my journal? Well, I just did.

CHAPTER FOUR
Childhood Revisited

Friday, March 31, 2023
Beyond Performance: A Blessed Spot

I realized as I played "Romance D'Amor" for Bernice, especially the second section, making my usual flubs and mistakes in the difficult barre measures, that I would never, ever be able to play classical guitar in public. A lifelong dream of constant practice to reach perfection smashed. Quite a shock.

But it is post-Covid time, and I am ready for the transformation pay-off shocks. Okay, what does never playing for the public ever mean? I have come up with the answer: Do it for fun and fascination. So, on to beyond performance.

Yes, I will still *appear* in public. But I won't *be* in public. It's vaguely scary. Slipping into the secret, hidden, mystery of life with its silent, unknown scents, and strange visions.

Guitar in a Kabbalah Frame of Mind

This means the warring factions of sloppy and perfect cease fighting. Their struggle falls away, doesn't matter, disappears. Both warriors unite in a space beyond performance. That's where the fun starts! The audience slides away, disappears. Thank God for that! And yes, now the Lord and I are working directly together. This *is* a blessed spot! There's nothing left but fun and a bit of fascination.

Saturday, April 1, 2023
The Kabbalah Way

I'm upset because household guests will disturb my peace and focus. But why should they? Change nothing. Simply add a bit to the core. Keep my peace and focus in the midst of the storm. It's the Kabbalah way. Also good time to practice and deepen Kabbalah. Have fun and fascination with household guests.

How to Turn Drudgery into Gold

Is there fun and fascination in making a bed? Probably somewhere. But how and where to find it? What is the secret of turning drudgery into gold? Only through the creative of imagination.

Monday, April 3, 2023
Slow-Growth Boundaries

Kabbalah has always been about poetic truth. For guitar, this involves a new individual (golem) born out of the raw clay of Milan, Sor, and Tarrega (beyond the classics). Push too far beyond my daily clay golem, slow-growth allotment boundaries, and I get nauseous.

Tuesday, April 4, 2023

Gematria is somewhat poetic and so clever. But is it true? Or a mental game of imagination? Deepening through numbers, letters, Pythagoras, and musical notes.

Thursday, April 6, 2023
Cholam Day: Once the Dam Breaks, There's No Going Back!

Cholam Day is beauty—mercy, forgiveness, and strength day. Today is my guitar Cholam Day: It begins by having mercy on myself, forgiving myself for sloppy guitar playing with its so-called "mistakes." But ultimately, this means forgiving myself for my strengths, for my power.

What does such forgiveness mean?

Since I don't believe in guilt, I don't feel guilty about my strengths but rather worried, fearful that, if I display them, I'll be slapped down. This started even before concert audiences and critics, when, at around age seven, for the first time over a small disagreement, I stood up to my mother. Her response: "Don't you dare! I'll slap you down!"

Evidently, that was a turning point. I never spoke up or stood up to her again. During future confrontations anywhere, I responded by simply smiling, inwardly or outwardly, and retreated into the safety of my inner world. To this day, that's the way I handle most negative situations. Never a direct confrontation, always an instinctive retreat, a stepping back. Often it's to my advantage.

It gives me space, time to analyze the situation and respond more diplomatically when I finally do. Nevertheless, the drawback is a hesitation about admitting, even knowing my own strengths.

But guitar-wise, those days are over. If, while playing, I forgive myself for my strength and forgive Ma for awkward displays of her power, I can release a mighty flow of energy that will bring powerful guitar playing.

Friday, April 7, 2023

Today Cholam, with the power to forgive (equaling beauty) taken for granted, I've crossed that bridge and am never going back!

The glimmer of audience is creeping in. Overpower them with

the cholam of Milan's "Pavane in C" beauty!

Al Hambra is saying, "Overpower the audience with thumb power, strength, merciful, and forgiveness beauty. I'm so grateful and happy that I forgave myself. No problem. Larry Leyenda still can't believe how good things are. But he's coming around. These childhood friends will soon play together again!

What about Sam Sor? Where does he fit in? He's happy too but doesn't yet know why. Can he stand all this happiness? Next thing is getting used to it. All these childhood friends are playing together again (John Berwald, John Mayer, and me).

Is that where I'm headed now? The next direction? Back to childhood, Riverdale, the farm? Not a bad place to go. Write children's stories like Dr. Seuss and Pop.

Playing reinforcements at the fountain in Park Ewen (age five or six) were the happiest moments of my life. That's where happiness was revealed.

Other happy moments:

1. Violin soaring in my room (age 15 or 16).
2. Conducting: preparing to conduct Rossini's "Overture" for the Music and Art High School orchestra, standing in the mirror in Miki's room watching my conducting moves, trying to copy David Zimmerman's conducting technique. Exciting. (Age 16.)

This shows an early *positive* view of audience. I was somehow unafraid and loving it: conducting; later, in the form of leadership, social directing, etc. Love of audience—no problem. Not even an issue or mention. Same later with folk singing.

Only classical guitar messed it up. For years. What a mess. And I hate a mess.

Well, all that is coming to an end.

I'm at the door of audience-love rebirth.

Saturday, April 8, 2023
Compliments and Criticism

Compliments and criticism are the "same."

If I pay attention to either one, let the ego get involved, which it usually does, they throw me off and distract me from my guitar playing.

The idea is to stay focused. That's the main thing. The rest, whether it be compliment or criticism, cloud or storm, is to be acknowledged, to give it some attention—but then I have to move on and focus on the main event, playing guitar.

Sagacity Comes to Jimmy: Leading the Sefirotic Life

The sefirot have poetic value. Their meanings are interpreted by the sages, who, through imagination, have created kabbalistic traditions of meaning, interpretations of the Tree of Life. Not a bad thing to do. I stand with the sages. Since I'm now old enough and have developed my own sagacity, why not interpret the sefirot in my own way? Why not *be* one of the sages? How bold is that!

Here's my own *nekudic* interpretation: the diacritic *segol* represents the trinity.

What is my next bold step? Leading the sefirotic life. It starts with Sage Guitar playing, which for me begins with the Milan "Pavane" C chord, the center of the universe. When I play that opening chord, a new world is born. And once the chord is created, I play on to create more notes, more worlds.

The trinity of kabbalah, sefirot, and guitar meet in the C chord.

"Alhambra" begins in A minor, which is the relative minor of C. These relatives are part of my family. Sor's "Etude No. 12" is in A major. A cousin. A is also the head of the neighboring Alphabet family. We're longtime friends, and, although not related, they're part of my family. So I create a new world with each note I play. What a responsibility! All those children! Thousands of individuals, little mental golems running out of my guitar. Am I releasing savages into the world? Or lovers? I'd prefer lovers. Then play on and create them! Maybe a combo would be good: Savage lovers! Yes, I like that.

Sunday, April 9, 2023

My *netivot* are tired. Time to step back and absorb them a bit. Make up my own *netivot*. Maybe this is the choreographic, creative, personal answer, as with kabbala. *My own interpretation.* "Inter," between; "pret," spread; "ation" ending.

Trying to fit my guitar playing into other people's interpretations is, however, both impossible and a total lie.

Truth is, I can *only* do it my way. No matter how hard I try to fit, to be or play like others, it cannot be done. The journey may be lonely, but it is impossible to be anything but unique.

The Last Stronghold Has Fallen

If there is anything to regret in life, it is that I have not had the courage to play classical guitar as my true self. I've gotten close in all the other areas. Classical guitar is the last stronghold. ("Alhambra" is its last redoubt.)

Blowing up this last stronghold of inauthenticity has been my practice goal. It's falling now.

Trembling with Power: A Finger Earthquake

As I reach out with my thumb, crossing as I stretch my hypothenar bridge toward my "Alhambra" string, see how my thumb trembles with formerly hidden, but now slowly emerging, unleashed power.

Monday, April 10, 2023
Being a Believer

The spokes of the wheel all lead to the hub, the center. Pain and (the choice of) suffering are embodied in the means (body) or instruments (paths). Glory and freedom are found at the Center.

How to answer my constant questions about meaning and purpose? When unanswered, these questions always lead to depression. So when feeling lost, down, drifting, and alone, I must center myself in mysticism, metaphysics, and the Higher Power. This means that, although the spokes of my wheel are many, at the center, I am a believer because *being a believer works!*

Mission Accomplished

When I pluck the index finger, my hypothenar muscle and thumb pull away; they move in parallel directions. They work together.

Does my conscious knowledge and recognition of this mean something? Anything? Yes! Knowing it gives index and thumb *added strength*. And yes, it helps even out the notes, straighten things up. It definitely works!

In fact, the kabbalistically parallel powers of male (thumb) and female (index, as leader of all the fingers) working together in my hand, uniting the world, may be the greatest discovery ever! Celestial forces, that is, although opposites, pull together in parallel directions.

So, today's guitar results: I've got it. That's it. Best ever! Just do it! (Followed, needless to say, by a sudden hesitancy, a fear of bringing so brilliant a discovery to light (to the public, i.e., audience squelch and dimming view. But that fear is dead and gone).

Tuesday, April 11, 2023

History is drifting in, and I'm afraid that language is drifting out. Afraid? That like violin, language study will wither and die?

Well, so what? Maybe language, especially Hebrew study, has served its primary purpose. I chose Hebrew for the connection with bible study and the Higher Power. I am now a believer. Also, I have cracked the "Alhambra" code. Now I am a prisoner of doubt—an upgraded prison. Still, I am happy about my index finger freely flying and displaying herself among the Doubters.

Should father impose more family discipline? Or let Index fly about freely for a bit longer? I vote for a bit longer. Let her shine!

The above entry, with its realizations about losing Hebrew and unifying song and classics in fictional characters, three art forms combined, has knocked me out in a wave of fatigue and depression. I have lost Hebrew and the mental separation-of-art-forms, which I have always hated. So although all this is an advance, it also feels like a loss. Evidently, every advance has a loss within it. Tears water progress and the future.

Wednesday, April 12, 2023
The Guitar Family

I'm returning to pre-violin and pre-guitar times, reinventing my childhood in a guitar light. It's a more convincing day. The sun stays bright even while the half-sliver moon comes out. Father Al not only has a day job, he *is* a day job. He has to keep his thumb-sun shining while his moon-fingers remain small, present, but almost hidden.

Larry, too. Yes, Uncle Larry is convinced, too. What about the children—Sam, Sarah, and the others? They all go out to play. But where is Mama? Could she be Mrs. Folk Song? (And Mrs. Folk Dance?) How surprising would that be!

Sarah (Gavotte-en-Rondeau) just finished playing in her sandbox. While playing, she works out her A minor depression. In the end, she's calm, tranquil, and bordering on happy.

Meanwhile Sam is playing reinforcements at the fountain across the street in Park Ewen.

CHAPTER FIVE

Belief Works

Thursday, April 13, 2023
Belief Works! Beauty. . .and Truth

Despair is a feeling, not an option.

Deep within each doubt, past the despair, helplessness, despondency, and anger, is the decision to go forward, to do it anyway, despite obstacles.

That decision is the reward.

Friday, April 14, 2023

I'm in a cross-over, fuck-it-all mode with my guitar. Screw the past and all its mumblings. Start off the morning with a fuck-it-all Milan "Pavane." Caution, care, and exactness out the window. Throw out months, years, of inhibition. Let the mighty thumb and shoulders roll! Tension and muscle tightness be damned! This is a great place to be. Dump it and fly with the wind.

Saturday, April 15, 2023
Reaching Out

Reaching out is not a big deal. It's part of the process and happens easily and naturally—but until now, it hasn't been so with classical guitar, and certainly not part of "Alhambra," in which reach-out-resistance has been located in my thumb and hypothenar region with its avoidance of bass as melody.

But that period of guitar playing is ending, and the reaching out, the emphasizing, displaying, opening up, and showing the bass, are becoming part of the "Alhambra." *And the more I reach out, the easier it gets!*

If the universe is created by the metaphorical speech of God, how does this relate to guitar playing? Play equals fun equals creation. When I play guitar, with each note I play, think I am diving into the center of creation, the center of the universe. I am living in the moment, bringing forth a new world with each note I play. Am I playing "other people's music" when I play compositions by other composers?

Not really. Truth is, it's no longer their music when I play it. Rather I'm putting fleshy sound on the skeleton of tradition they left. I'm building the house, and adding the spirit of life to their (sometimes ancient) architectural plans.

Sunday, April 16, 2023
A Key Guitar Date: Al's Different Place

Low wrist, and low, relaxed tip of the thumb—not the meat of it: an immediate fast. Precarious balance, but right.
Accept it as *right!* Yes!
Finally, a *yes!*
Now *solidify my (new) base by enjoying it!*
Luxuriate in my new thumb!

Audience

I glimpsed it in my mind. I can, with my new thumb, actually play "Alhambra" before an audience. Yes, I am right! This is the way! Astonishing. I am there. Calm yourself, I say!

Monday, April 17, 2023
Be Fruitful and Multiply: The Kick-Ass Life

I am tired of weeping, wailing, moaning, complaining, giving in, giving out, slithering, and sliding.

Let me adopt a kick-ass lifestyle instead compounded of equal measures of passion and compassion, and bits of love and beauty. And I'll have a winner.

Start with kick-ass guitar. Then move on to kick-ass folk dancing, and from there, expand it to kick-ass the rest of my life.

How did I come to this conclusion?

This morning, after reading about how yesod, the foundation of the kabbalistic Tree of Life, symbolizes the biblical commandment "be fruitful and multiply," and that this commandment also means multiplying your good deeds, I asked myself, what good deeds can I do?

Play guitar for others jumped into my mind. This was followed by the "obvious," folk dancing. But it's the Mosaic leadership commandment I have been avoiding for over forty exiled years. Am I ready to listen now? A trembling burning bush says *yes*.

First Chords

Milan's "Pavane in C"—striving for a good deed. Send out healing vibrations to all, the audience a prayer. Will it work? In miracle fashion, maybe. By sending small vibrations, I might channel the Mighty vibrations. Together we might accomplish something. Does prayer work? It might. Why not simply assume it does? This means my guitar playing would have an effect. Even long-distance. When its vibrations are focused, they can help others.

Next I'd send a special delivery gift of belief in a totally relaxed thumb along with a melodious bass, followed by a high-powered, just-have-fun delivery.

Finally, comes the kick-ass, "smash 'em with the log of your choice," the grand message. Maybe tomorrow I'll send a Bach kick-ass "Gavotte en Rondeau." Good for a fresh beginning.

Tuesday, April 18, 2023
Humble Road

Last night I healed myself *through* my folk dance class. My dancers "forced" me to be better, pushing me—through my commitment to them—to heal myself, to promote, bring out, fulfill, heal, to become my better, even best, self. They forced this shy, resistant teacher out from hiding in the closet, dragged me into the open, and in the process healed me.

Thank you, my dancers! Thank you, work. Thank you that I'm "forced" to perform, to rise above my narrow, cowardly, ever-hiding negative self, squeezed out of the tube into my better self, and am able to fulfill the dictates, wishes, and promises of my best self. My folk dance class forces me to be better. And, as I teach it, I became better. Thank God for my work! But what *is* my work? Dealing with, helping others, raising their spirits. In the process, I heal myself.

Can I heal myself organizing and selling tours? Only two people have registered for the Bulgarian tour. I'm afraid that, once they find out how small the "group" is, they'll cancel. And will our guide Ventsi even run the tour with only two? Probably. If I put in maximum effort for the next two weeks, commit myself to selling this Bulgarian tour, will it heal me? Probably.

I hate making the effort. Seems I start most "work" things that way. I resist with every cell of my being. Yet "luckily" my hatred of humiliation is greater than my resistance to effort. So I'll do it in spite of the negatives. If I have any success, I feel glorious! That is the grand payoff. Humble Road is up ahead. (Why

"*Humble* Road?" Where did that word come from? What does it mean?)

Wednesday, April 19, 2023

Humility exists to help you realize where your powers are and to make you stronger.

Guitar

Thumb comes to "Pavane in C" and on C. Doubt is crushed by belief. Everywhere thumb appears, it will be different. It will be spread throughout the universe. Get used to it. Glory to thumb! Thumb normal at 95% light. (Treble almost silent at 5% shadow.) Fingers equal little bits of ego; thumb as Father, the Universal. Let treble disappear for a while. (Olam and hidden.)

Thursday, April 20, 2023

I am a perfectionist. I strive to get better to reach this ultimate goal. I hate imperfection. But except for a few glorious moments, perfection is unreachable. Happiness will come when I can accept imperfection. It's human to be imperfect. But who wants that?

My wife says perfection is irrelevant. No doubt she is realistic and right. Are realism and right the way to go?

Here's a new angle: Love the fact that I will never be able to play "Alhambra," and that, because of this, it keeps pushing me, inspiring me to continue practicing and playing my beloved guitar. If not for this endless and perpetual challenge, I might never play. So thank this endless frustration and pleasure. Enjoy my imperfections. They keep me traveling on the challenging, smiling road of improvement.

Graduation Day

Mother Vulture said, "A wise old bird once told me, 'When you learn to fly, you can't avoid pain. But suffering is a choice.'"

"I like that," answered Hector, sitting on the edge of the nest. "And I agree. I'm trying to fly, but it hurts. Fog in the sky. Rough nest edges, and growing pains in my wing-spread, are the biggies. But other annoying growth spurts are aching me, too."

"You're a strange bird," Mother Vulture ventured, cleaning a feather with her beak. "But that's why I hatched you."

"All my nest life, this stuff has ruffled my feathers," Hector continued. "Part of me glories in the challenge. I feel like my own hero, tolerating the unbearable, working through each obstacle. But on the other foot, part of me hates to admit weakness. Suffering is for losers."

"Not exactly true," Mama Vulture pointed out. "It's your choice. Attitude is all."

Hector attempted a flutter. His small wing rose, moved to the right, hung there for a moment, then collapsed. He sighed, then gave up. He glanced at the sky and uttered a squawk of displeasure. "Why do I have to choose it?"

"Easy," Mother Vulture flapped. "She's a good teacher. Suffering, I mean."

"She? Or he? I'm into fowl pronouns. And is it Ms. Suffering or Mrs.?"

"These distinctions are superficial and unimportant."

"Okay. As for teachers, I like to have good ones. But is there a less painful way to learn? Will there ever be a time when I graduate from suffering and move on to higher degrees?"

"There's a graduate Ph.D. program in the Vulture Division of Paine College."

"My sister told me about that before you pushed her out of the nest last week."

"I never pushed. She decided to leave on her own."

"Well, in any case, I'm not interested."

Mother remained silent.

Moments later Hector asked, "Do I really need a doctorate from Vulture School to graduate?"

A week later, he asked, "Do I even want to graduate? . . ."

"I think so."

After months of cogitation vulture-style, he asked, "But how does one graduate?"

Time passed. A year later, as parts of the nest began to rot, bits of sallow wisdom crept in. "Well," he concluded, "since suffering is a choice, graduating from it is also a choice. No one can *give* me a degree. I have to do it myself. Am I ready? Probably. Do I want it now? Probably. . . ." He slapped a strong wing against the nest. "Actually, my answer is *definitely*. I'm just not ready to admit it."

Another month passed. "Well, maybe I am. What's the next step?

"Accept claw and beak aches," said his mother, "wing aches, too. But give up *suffering*.

"Really? Reject such a good friend? We've been through so much nesting together. Is it time to say goodbye? Can I live without it?"

At that point, Mother Vulture's sister flew by. Fluttering around the edges of the nest, she squawked, "Go, my nephew. Fly away. Freedom time has come. I'm pushing you out. The next pain you feel will be your head crashing into a rock at the bottom of our neighborhood abyss. (Why your mother built her nest on a cliff, I'll never know.) Once you hit the ground, just rub your head and start walking. Flying will begin right after your first step."

Two days later Hector called up to his mother from an oak tree branch in the abyss below.

"Thanks, Ma. I always needed a push."

She laughed. "You may have *wanted* one, my bird, but you never *needed* one. And I wouldn't give you one, even if you begged me."

"But Ma—"

"Don't 'Ma' me. You'll notice you're the one who pushed yourself out. That's why you shouted 'Goodbye' on your way down."

"But. . .but now I'm beginning to miss you."

"Another lie. Just shut up, get off that branch, take a step, and fly."

A week later Hector found himself in Istanbul.

Friday, April 21, 2023
Play Guitar My Way

A big advantage to age and aging is: It slows you down. And for me, that's a good thing. I make most of my mistakes by rushing, moving too fast. Added to this, ancient ghosts in my brain daily create an internal pressure to move fast, speed up, do things quickly. Somehow, in my personal mythology, moving fast equates macho and smart.

How this happened may be traced to my childhood upbringing, in which the message was that slow equaled stupid. "You're so slow," was a withering put-down. Hearing it knocked the wind and spirit out of me. So for years, I strove for fast and ran from slow.

Of course this attitude haunts my classical guitar playing, creating a constant grand inferiority sanctification. I freeze when I play fast, feel incompetent and inferior, but still refuse to slow down. It adds up to an imperfect classical guitar life.

What to do about imperfection? What is left but to enjoy it? *Relish* imperfections, even attempts at improvement. The pressure to play fast is my nemesis. *To slow down is my challenge.* Tempi, slow or fast, are *techniques*.

I played again. Slow, loose, relaxed. I enjoyed it. What is the result of these post-Covid musings? My inferiority complex sems to have run its ancient course. Exhausted and fading, it's no longer needed. Give it up. Play guitar *my way*. What is my way? Slow . . .and beautiful! How beautiful when I slow down and luxuriate in the rich sound of gorgeous and glorious notes.

Saturday, April 22, 2023

Mr. Focus has power. I'm jealous. I want it. . .but I hesitate to take it. He appears in my slow and beautiful guitar playing. If I accept this power, will I lose my audience? It's okay with me if I do. Truth is, though, I'll never lose my audience. Only some of them. A select few will always stick around.

Sunday, April 23, 2023
Introduction

As humans we have to go through the Give-It-All-Up barrier to reach the land of Glory. As you slide off the perfection ladder, it's the first step up. Pushing (slightly) beyond limits creates exhilaration.

Can I? Motivation from doubt comes from desire to prove yourself.

Mama, can you love a slow index finger? (I doubt it. But I will work toward it, hoping I am wrong and that some day I can win your love. How sad, vulnerable, human, and true. Is to be human pathetic? "Pathetic" is a put-down, a fancy word to avoid humanity and admitting vulnerability. To be human, we all need love and nurturing at any age, and always. Cry for the beauty and humanity of it!

Deep in my imagination, Mama is my audience. Every index finger pluck needs her love, approval, and nurturing. Will she give it? If she does, can I take it? Ask my imagination.

Monday, April 24, 2023
I Am Stronger in Guitar and Folk Dancing

Most surprising and shocking is the possibility of my new strength. I've gotten stronger in folk dancing and guitar. Of course, this is "reasonable" since, especially since January, I've been spending hours working aerobically at the gym at the treadmill, bicycle and scifi machine (along with weights) and, daily, practicing right-hand guitar tremolo and more technique.

Nevertheless, this sudden demonstration of progress in strength and aerobic fitness surprises me. We did some fast folk dances yesterday, which, a few months ago, caused me to huff, puff, and give up in fear of heart stuff. This time I breezed through each one. No problem—except for my own shock of happy amazement.

Meanwhile, my guitar playing, as notes in previous entries indicate, has been moving along steadily, passing through its "slow playing" state and finally reaching focus on the Beautiful.

Intellectually, I know the above is all true. But can I believe it *emotionally*? I *want* to. Dare I? I've learned that belief works, and that doubt has its own "prove it!" motivational force. I may simply need more time to quell my doubts and *prove* I am stronger. But I already have! So what's the big deal? I tremble at the thought. Yet it is true. Months of effort worked!

The Higher Focus Intensity Feeling

Would the pleasure of higher-focus intensity be enough of a reason to inspire me to "play" for an audience? To actually perform? Some call it "buzz." What a question! Truth is, pursuit of this feeling, the "pleasant uplift" of high intensity buzz, is the only reason I'd ever "want" to perform. Would I ever want it so badly, I'd look for a performance venue? (Amazing I'm even saying this.)

Saturday, April 29, 2023

Cracked the code. First day ever. Bring my own way of playing to the world. Some disabled notes may need some extra time to move, and that's okay. Part of the Kindness Program that Jim Gold brings to the show.

What's a kindness guitar? It starts with asking myself, Am I kind? Do I have a kindness *aspect*? The words "kind" or "kindness" have never been part of my vocabulary. I almost never use them. But perhaps they have been a *hidden* part, especially of my classical guitar-playing life.

Of course, for the first time in memory, I'm being kind to myself by allowing myself play guitar my own way. If I am in this fashion kind to *myself*, kindness will naturally flow out to others, flow through my fingers and be expressed.

If I am kind to myself, I can also have fun with myself. And like kindness, the fun will naturally flow out to others. It all starts with the self. Being kind on the instrument leads to fun.

Sunday, April 30, 2023
Guitar

Through the Milan "Pavane in A," I am pouring wisdom into the world. It's my first outward move from an integrated place. (Well, *inching* toward outward, anyway.)

I am moved, in the three Milan "Play" Pavanes, by the simplicity and depth of their nekkudim.

What is so curious and interesting about my index finger? It is ever pointing and searching. I feel like so much of my former "personality" is going out the window. The index finger points to the Imagination, and vice versa. It's deep in my fingers meaty, fleshy, and fun!

A fun "Gavotte en Rondeau" is my next step. I need to push all the wisdom I've got. But it means fun and wisdom are within my realm. This is quite amazing and wonderful. I need to give myself the privilege of dwelling in happy wonder and amazement for a while.

CHAPTER SIX

Stranger than Fiction: Love and Helping Others

Wednesday, May 3, 2023

The opposite of fear is safety.

Last Rites of Guitar Self-Analysis

Soft and slow can be fun. It is a good warm-up mode. Fast and clear come next. Stratospheric playing, though, has its danger point. Use the fear in a positive way.

Danger and fear, comfort and calm: Neither is better, just different. In the world of difference, there is no value judgement.

Thursday, May 4, 2023
Perfection

Perfection resides in the mind. Created by the imagination, it is a path, not a destination. Walk the path. Give up the illusion that it's anything more.

Goals Accomplished: Mere Enjoyment

"Mere enjoyment" is a gift, an achievement. I like it. . .for a while. But the adjective "mere" points to emptiness, chaos, and the abyss that follows reaching a goal. In this realm, enjoyment is pleasant and serves as a mild form of motivation stimulant. But it's not enough. A by-product reward, it lies on the sideline of creation. Inspiration, passion, enthusiasm work better.

This is all a sweet way of saying: I need some fresh artistic and spiritual goals.

Friday, May 5, 2023
Love and Helping Others

In riding a directionless and confused emotional state into love, help others and do what's right. Love is the feeling; doing what's right is the act. Love breaks up and scatters old world-views.

Does my guitar playing (and the other stuff I do) help the weak? I need to think and believe it does. Imagine it into being. Make it so. The whole enterprise of love and helping others is a totally unfamiliar way for me of looking at my guitar playing and everything else I do.

The index finger is the love finger. It points to the love path and its act of helping others. I'd even say not knowing this has been holding me back all these years from *expressing* love and helping others through my guitar. Folk dancing and tours, too.

Love gives you the power to do what's right. It lifts you beyond fight-or-flight, bypasses ego, is stronger than fear.

Saturday, May 6, 2023
Raging Soul, Raging Prayer, Returning with Fire

Can rage be a prayer? Why not? Rage boils the fish in the kettle. So it leads to the Kingdom. Passionate prayer ignites the soul, while study calms its waters. So resurrect my raging soul.

I feel better already!

Sunday, May 7, 2023
Clouds and Sun: The Sparkless Existence

I have goals but no spark. The heart of them has shriveled away. The sun has been blocked by clouds. It's temporary, yes, but what to do? Dive into the lifeless, sparkless pond of old goals. Do them anyway! I know the right path. I'm on it. Sparks, like clouds, come and go. Say hello, then move on without them. It's okay, even good!

Go over my past in total depth. Make a renaissance of it. The fact is, I can't go back to the old life. Okay, time to fix my mind, straighten out its desires, realize *I don't want to* go back to that life! It had lots of put-downs, a miserable "Alhambra," lots of self-smashing. My current life has little to no self-smashing, lots of confidence, is not miserable, has a happy "Alhambra," a happy "Leyenda" on its way, and happy guitar playing in sight!

Monday, May 8, 2023
Promised Land

"What is the guitar promised land?" Jack asked Martha as they sat in the garden, munching on a chocolate chip cookie.

Martha reached for her apple juice. "For you," she answered, "it's performing in front of an audience."

Jack pulled a lemon out of his knapsack, bit into it, and sucked with vengeance. "Somehow I will not perform." Clouds floated above him. He grimaced. "More disturbing is that I don't want to."

Trees trembled in their roots. Martha emitted a sardonic laugh. "Process is more curious than product. Even our neighbor Dan Satin agrees." She sipped her juice. "Except for paradise," she went on. "Once you reach the top, succeed, and achieve your earthly goals, after a brief *wahoo* you get itchy. I know you, Jack. Wait too long after you arrive, and you begin to run around smashing flowers, tearing leaves off trees, pulling vegetables out of the ground, fruit trees by the roots, and screaming 'What's next, what's neat?' Seems, even in this lovely garden, standing still is not an option."

"Could it be I like failure better than success?" Jack said. "Is walking somewhere better than arriving?"

"It's different for sure. As for better or worse, let the Big Guy handle the moral questions."

"Perhaps it's impossible for me to embrace success. I'll only dream about it but never do it."

"Could be."

"Impossible dreams never dissatisfy."

"Our neighbor says that dissatisfaction is the lot of man."

"I know, Jack. He uses two 'a's in his name."

CHAPTER SEVEN

Postscript

Wednesday, May 10, 2023
The Grand Tickle

Soft guitar playing only attracts those ready to listen. Loud playing hits the audience over the head, grates on the ear, forces folks to *hear* you but not necessarily *listen*.

Loud is different from strong. I may never go back to the way I was on the guitar. I may never play Sor's "Etude No. 12," or any other piece in my repertoire, that fast again. The old fast may be a way of the past. Is there a new one?

Thursday, May 11, 2023
The Guitar Story: Escape from Slavery

I love the power, confidence, and strength in my new index finger. It has its own iron box of three steel-tipped fingers, independent and confident. This iron box is my heritage, my right, and I claim it. I never want to go back to slavery.

Why do we love stories of escape from slavery? Because we're imprisoned in our bodies, ever trying to reach the land of our dreams. That's what the guitar story is all about. Francisco Tarrega is my Moses of guitar. His children of Israel are fingers, "Alhambra" the Promised Land, index finger the walking stick to get there.

Saturday, May 13, 2023
Lonely? How to Eliminate Feeling Alone?

I lead tours, folk dancing, folk song group singing, and I have been a hotel social director. I didn't, and don't, have a problem with any of them. In high school, I conducted the Music and Art

High School orchestra. Also no problem. But being a soloist has caused big problems for me.

In the profound nature of language, using the right words is important. Using the wrong ones can confuse and mess you up.

I feel comfortable with words like "leader" and "conductor." I rebel against "soloist." It's too lonely, alienating, and dictatorial.

Of course, I could reinterpret the etymology of "solo" by relating it to "sun" (one), soul (soul-o-ist), sole (of the foot). Yes, I'm twisting the etymology of "solo" to fit my needs. But perhaps that's okay. "Everyone" does it. Twisting things to fit your mind is the way of the world.

Fun Sephira

Speaking of the world, in the Kabbalah world, what is the *fun* sephira? It must be the crown (keter), since it unites all. The problem is: I feel alone (and somewhat lonely) in my fun. How can I change that? A common answer is to share my fun with the audience.

But I hate the word "share." It comes from the root "shear," which means to cut, separate, partition, divide. I hate division; I love union.

So it's totally the wrong word for me. I *hate* division, and sharing is division *par excellence!* I don't want to shear the audience away from me.

I love togetherness. I want to move beyond divisive moments and toward unification. Uniting is one unit, and one unit equals one. Uniting in union is the only way to go. All is One is the nature of the crown.

Breaking the Audience–Soloist Choke Hold

I may have broken the audience–soloist choke hold. This means I could lead or conduct an audience. A huge deal.

Monday, May 15, 2023
Sunday Night Dread Eliminated

The fear of Monday morning, with its financial and worldly challenges, used to haunt my Sunday evenings. But now somehow, this ancient Sunday night dread has disappeared. Nice!

From Product to Process

I will never be a finished product until *I* am finished, as a product, and become a process. Better is to think of self, and my art forms, as an unfinished process than as a finished product.

The Fun, Flying Fingers-on-Fire Kabbalah: Guitar "Technique"

Segol, as the three-fingers-in-one tremolo, could be the fun sephira, the fun-one finger. (Very) soft *segol,* in the distance, with *malkut* (and a bit of *yesod*) beating out thumb-pounding rhythm and melody at the bottom. The fingers-on-fire kabbalah—that's the one I want!

My enthusiasm for folk dancing started to disappear when I stopped choreographing folk dances and began a retreat into more "traditional" programming. Note "retreat." Evidently, I must be creative (choreo) or I lose interest in dancing.

Tuesday, May 16, 2023
Freedom and Slavery

For years "Alhambra" held me prisoner. I was a happy slave, tied to my inability to play it. This lack filled my mind with determination and purpose to conquer this Tarrega tremolo masterpiece. But now that I've accepted *my* way of playing guitar, the slavery is over. "Suddenly," after three years of Covid retreat and practice, I'm a free man! The dawn rose in April. Stunned and pleased, I celebrated and I absorbed the sunlit possibilities.

Today I have arrived. The tightening in my chest—weak, aching, stiff, hesitant, and fearful—tells me I'm ready to move on. Yes, after celebration comes the chaotic and loss-filled *now what?* I'm beginning my flight over the abyss. Jean Paul Sartre said that freedom is the ability to chose your form of slavery. Do I need a revised form of it?

CHAPTER EIGHT

Performance Life Workbook

Wednesday, May 17, 2023

I'm in a frame of mind I don't think I've been in before. It feels neutral—no strong feelings, treading water, holding in place, with vague to no anxiety—waiting, waiting. It's not a *neighborhood* at all. Rather a sort of bus stop.

I hope it is a gestation place. But here even "hope" is absent. Any seeds? So far, only Zoom.

Maybe, in this strange locale, the next me is being (or has already been) born. This infant self looks around with fresh eyes. The world seems different.

I suspect that my Performance Life self has ended, along with the seemingly endless monastic Covid retreat.

During this three-year "vacation," I put things together and in order. Now it's time to return to work, and finish the job.

What *is* the job? Bringing my stuff to the public. Helping to heal the world. I have a natural resistance to leaving the soft life and returning to the workaday. The resistance is real but futile. Like a child returning from a wonderful summer vacation who has no choice but to return to school in September, I am facing my September. How do I do it?

Avoid the three distractions:

1. The jealousy distraction (others play guitar, etc., better than I do). It's a pretty powerful one. I must remember that, like everybody else, I'm unique, and I have a unique style and purpose.
2. The inferiority distraction—another excuse not to focus on my path.
3. The lost-and-lack-of-purpose distraction. Truth is, I am *not*

lost; I *know* my purpose. So I have to focus on the task at hand and dive in.

Meditations on Performance and Purpose

Having finished my meditations on it, and standing at the edge of the abyss of performance, ready to jump off the cliff, I'm wondering: Do I want to?

Maybe my purpose is not to perform.

Maybe purpose has nothing to do with performing, and vice versa.

Maybe I have no purpose; maybe there *is* no grand purpose in life. Maybe my only purpose, the only reason to play the guitar, is to give me something to do, to pleasantly (or unpleasantly) pass the time.

So though I've reached my goal, freed my mind of its obstacles, and I can now perform, I still don't *feel* like performing! How strange is the result, the conclusion of this Covid search. Maybe, aside from the basics for survival, I don't need a purpose. Maybe I don't need that much.

Friday, May 19, 2023
Without Hang-Ups

I used to love all this stuff—but something happened.

What?

I'm not sure. But whatever it is, or was, time to go back to my former miracle-schedule life—but this time *without the hang-ups*.

Yes, I'm returning fresh.

Maybe it's just a question of getting used to *living* without hang-ups—light and free. I've never done it.

Let the Excitement Linger

Another Greek tour registration just came in. Happy excitement! No need to confirm it right away. It won't disappear.

My Way

It was once unheard of for me to play guitar without hang-ups. Why is the road open now? I think it's because I'm finally playing it *my way*. And it occurs to me that this impulse to find a distinct, special-case-of-one path is both enormously powerful and true of everybody. Only the character of each path differs—for some people, it's all about an artistic or spiritual search. For others, it can be about making money or playing golf.

Getting to Know Mr. Gnue Qitarr

When I met Gnue Qitarr on Friday, he extended his right hand. "Please," he said.

Taken aback by such a remark, I at first hesitated. His right hand looked strong, dominant, powerful, with a prominent index pointing straight at me (into my heart), fingers dangling beneath them with a causal haughtiness—or was it confidence?—and thumb standing proud and straight, pointing to the sky. I just was not used to such dynamism, especially at a first meeting.

Noting my hesitancy, he softened. "Don't be afraid," he said, pulled back his hand, withdrew a nail buffer from the vest pocket of his tuxedo, polished the index nail, and, after adjusting his bow tie, extended his hand again. I shook it. "Just call me Gnue," he said.

I did, and that has made all the difference!

Monday, May 22, 2023
Different Reasons

Respect, confidence, pleasing others, money, fame, old fears and hesitancies, all of that, is dead. (Even self-improvement has paused as a motivation and is, in its old frantic form, probably dead as well.) They were killed off, during Covid time.

I'm not going anywhere, doing anything, and there is nothing I want. I am in neutral (but not neutered) state.

Can I discover different reasons to do the same miracle-schedule things I loved and still love to do? The first thing that comes to mind is boredom: I've got nothing else to fill up my time. I am very far from the stuff that fills most people's spells of dreariness.

So I picked up the guitar.

Some somatic psychology observations:

1. There's a real connection between my index finger and my lower back.
2. When my thumb plucks second string, then a finger plucks first, I sense a closeness and hesitancy (a sort of claustrophobia).

I'm "playing around" with purpose. Can playing "like a child" be a purpose? But what else is there? Could this lower-back sensation be a vital spot in the nervous system, a play center?

"Soleares" and "Leyenda" are my next adventures in mastery. And note how I like the *challenge* of this kind of a music war game.

Does this mean purpose, and the search for it, are only a game? What about the grand purpose, the beauty and motivational power of design, a mighty meaning, a life-changing goal? Are *they* only a game? If so, how disappointing.

And note, importantly I think, how I feel the disappointment in my lower back!

Wednesday, May 24, 2023
Humor in a Post-Performing Life

I'm getting sick of tragedy, sadness, and pain. Of course, these miseries will not disappear just because I'm sick of them. They are a fact of life and remain so whether I like them or not.

I only have control of my attitude; only my *approach* to these "facts" can change.

Here's a new one: We die, and that makes life pretty tragic, sad, and painful. But suppose we don't. Suppose there is more than just our body, mind, friends, family, neighbors, community, country, civilization, and world? Suppose there is more.

Suppose dying is just an annoyance—not really an ending, but a new beginning? What then?

Instead of choosing pain and suffering, can I let my sense of humor deal with these? Should I, as I try putting my Performing Life into practice, try writing humor? Working on it, seeing fantasy and humor as a craft, a skill, something *serious* that might be fresh and good for me? And surely it is worthy, a way to fight death and transience with fun.

In fact, this may be its only challenge! Humor is a love and talent I have. Crazy fictions and twists of reality, easily, often, and naturally pop into my head in both crazy and not-so-crazy situations.

But I have never developed this humor with its sense of the absurd. I've just "tossed it off" to forget about it. Obviously, it is one way I have of dealing with tragedy, sadness, and pain.

Certainly, pursued as a craft, it totally fits my post-Covid existence.

One purpose of writing my Performance Life journal has been to free myself from my old attitude toward performing, and maybe find another. Serious humor would fit that bill. Joy is an obvious component of it.

Thursday, May 25, 2023
Giving a Concert

I've wanted to give concerts again. Now I can. I can give myself one, each and every morning—a little concert with confidence and no hang-ups.

Friday, May 26, 2023
Folk Singing: The Final Cleansing

Embarrassed? Ashamed? Why? Of *my songs?* Yes.

When I return to my songs, my original creations, I feel shame. Time to clean up my creative and old folk song singing past attitudes.

I am embarrassed to just let go and release my love of beauty, to express it through the very personal art of folk singing.

What is embarrassment and shame but fear in disguise?

Okay, this hesitancy has, I admit, been a lifetime problem. Releasing it in private has been okay, just fine. But in public, and without the shield of humor, it's been a very difficult climb. At least for me. Let me explore this issue to see if I can make any sense of it.

Hidden behind the concept of folk songs as "inferior" is my *love* of these songs.

(Note, I feel no shame about opera or classical songs, since classical is always "superior.")

Another variation of this disease: Folk songs are *so simple and easy to play*, at least for me. That "proves" folk singing is an inferior art form, since I can so easily do it. This ridiculous snobbery (and that's what it is, nothing more) has protected me for years from releasing inner aspects of myself that express sadness, beauty, the magnificent meltdown, and glory.

How about *my* songs, the ones *I* have written, the originals? The instant the thought of these rises in my mind, I'm hit by an immediate *"Ugh!" That* is the creative "ugh self" core I need to eradicate. And I am. It's happening now. No wonder my legs are buckling, feel like they can't support me. My foundation is falling apart. This Covid monastery period is cleaning out a giant inferiority complex. No hiding anymore.

Tours, Study, and Business

I need to study India and Brazil to know about local Indian and Brazilian people. And I need to do the same with other languages.

Deepening my vision of these countries—*my* countries—from a distance (a Covid monastery effect) provides a fresh reason to study their geography, history, and languages. This will reinvigorate my tour studies on a new level, re-inspire and re-enthuse me.

1. I like and need study, in almost the same way in which I like and need business with its powerful money motive.
2. This adds the learning and excitement of study to my travel business and "from a distance," without traveling there, opens a new perspective.

Life among the Fingers

How is life among the fingers? Especially between the second and fourth of the left hand?

Well, second and fourth, when played, put, placed, stuck together, represent all the crippled people in the world. Crippled representatives need to stick up for the downtrodden. So they must be played, presented, in a certain way.

Which way? is the question.

And how do they feel about Fernando Sor? Do they like twisting and turning just to fit into his thirds in "Etude No. 12"?

Monday, May 29, 2023

Today is my birthday. So how should I begin? I'm tired of complaining about existential woes. I'm even a bit bored bringing them up and picking through them. They're always the same, repeating over and over again, *What is the meaning of my life? What is my cosmic purpose?*

The questions never get permanently answered. Only temporary help is available. And I always forget my daily transient answers, which enable me to plod ahead.

So the next day I start searching all over again, ending up with the same answers I arrived at the day before. Or simply forgetting yesterday's whole search with all the answers when I dive into the today's action.

This is a Sisyphean search *par excellence.*

Maybe I'm just scared—and a bit dazzled by the successes I'm achieving. Look at what I've accomplished. In the last few days, I've started running and singing again, classical guitar is moving along beautifully, and even a few new business ideas are popping up. All good stuff.

Yes, I'm dazzled by these accomplishments, and not used to, and certainly not good at, dealing with success. I'm used to the down life and a depressing frame of mind. I even (used to) like it! Like living submerged in a pit, I pushed myself daily to climb out of it. Every morning I awoke with a passionate desire to extricate myself, to climb up and out. And every day I did.

But now the illusion is gone. I don't accept its "reality" anymore. I believe in living in the present and dealing with the future by creating it. All good stuff.

Registration Is a Beautiful Thing

Another tour registration arrived in my email.
Registration validates everything.
And it makes me feel so good!
How to continue this upward path? Advertise and promote! Learn to love doing it! *Love it?* Well, why not?
What is a happy registration check but love in the mail? A blessing from above and below. One of the very best birthday presents.
Registration is a beautiful thing.

Would I increase self-love by giving a real concert to real people? Yes. (But it doesn't mean I will.)
Would I increase self-love by giving a real folk dance class to real people? Yes. And I already do.
How come? I'm set up for it.
I'm *not* set up for concerts. It would take a special effort to do that. Will I ever make the effort?
We'll see.
But I'm certainly not ready yet.

Birthday "Alhambra"

Another beautiful birthday gift is my "Alhambra." I need to accept it gratefully and gracefully.

That's self-love personified.

Will I soon, can I now, give this love to the world, the audience, the public?

Why should it take so long?

How about doing it today?

Wednesday, May 31, 2023
The Wonder of Depth

Depth, what Robert Frost called "the wonder of unexpected supply," results from a more focused life.

It means doing less, with fewer goals, which gives you space to dwell and time to sink down, linger there awhile, luxuriate in that wonder.

Al says, "No going back to ancient days. Guitar birthday time means loose and strong. Confidence comes with Finger Feeling. Dwell in the See chord. Linger in the power of its Beauty Pavane."

Thursday, June 1, 2023
Coming to Terms with Fear

Fear is a primal emotion.

Why would I ever consider throwing away such a jewel?

Writing is the gateway to self-knowledge and wisdom.

Therefore, where am I this morning?

Financial reckoning: I'm revisiting retirement. Can I really do it, and why?

I like exactness, perfection, knowing where I am.

Why have I not followed this model in my finances? Why do I stay blind and hoping, fly-by-the-seat-of-my-pants, ever keeping financial fears alive?

Part of it is to maintain my dreams of infinite riches (note: a dream I don't even need!). If I do it, I stay on my toes. In other words, it keeps my motivation cooking.

I'm happy and secure now in my "Alhambra." Are finances the next step? Are both together a package? Could be.

Fear keeps dreams of bliss, paradise, fearlessness, and infinite wealth alive. Retirement implies a fearless state. No wonder I resist it.

But I'm at the edge of a post-Covid method, with finances organized. I'll replace fear motivation with the beauty of accounting.

Will such beauty work?

I doubt I can say goodbye to fear. I have nothing to replace it with. That's the problem.

I only know fear as a source of motivation. And I *believe in it*, can't get rid of it.

Maybe I can't because it is a vital ingredient. Maybe *I need the motivation* it triggers. (That itself is scary.)

Maybe the blessed, fearless, paradisaical state I once sought is one I really *don't* want.

Okay—then, if fear so important, how can I employ it in a post-Covid life?

I used to see fear as unhealthy and weak. Now I'm not so sure. *Maybe it's healthy and strong to be afraid!* (But of course, not give *in* to it. I rarely do.)

Fun Fears

How about a month of exact finance, of watching my money? Would that be fearful and funny? Fearfully funny?

How about *fun fears*. Not a bad name.

After adding my monastic Covid attitude modifications, returning to pre-Covid levels isn't a bad place to be.

Saturday, June 3, 2023
Book Sales: On Improvement and Effort, A Commandment

By trying to improve, I end up with the satisfying process of elevation. Satisfaction is my reward. (Then it passes, and I try to win it again.)

If I don't make the effort, I feel miserable, sluggish, tired, depressed.

The choice is mine.

Monday, June 5, 2023

Commit to perfecting the body, and the soul will follow. This could be a big turning point for me. Running, yoga, Hebrew, and Torah sections (*parshas*), along with the fading likelihood of guitar and singing performances.

Add to this an acceptance and acknowledgment in public of my love of etymology and its vital importance in understanding history, geography, and more.

Tuesday, June 6, 2023
Torah and Guitar Combination

I seamlessly moved from Hebrew study into guitar this morning. Since performing has died, I'm looking for a reason to play guitar. Somehow it has to combine with Torah. To my secular brought-up mind, Torah means Jewish, and bible means secular.

In fact, Torah means *real* Jewish, orthodox, Hassidic Jewish, deep Jewish, extreme Jewish. Extremism is something I'm both attracted to and a bit afraid of.

What about Jewish guitar playing? Is there such a thing? For me? It's funny, a bit irreverent, and, in its humor, partly helps me avoid my Jewish roots, which I also admire.

Is there a Jewish "Alhambra"? Probably.

Deep Jewishness is part of the post-Covid Monastery self that is now emerging—my hidden connection to history, to my Abrahamic source.

And although my guitar connection is no longer to performing, to giving concerts, perhaps it will be to Jewishness. Could performing be part of that?

I am thus mixing soteriology and the spiritual, combining secular and religious, that is, into one. Could it ultimately be called "performing"?

Note how this reflects in the fingers, which, in the playing of Sor's "Etude No. 12," symbolize the secular and religious souls. When I play the opening "thirds" (two notes together), the secular and religious move up and down together. No problem. First and third finger are smooth, second and fourth fingers are squeezed, harder, rougher, tougher, but still doable. Putting secular and religious together is pretty much the same process. So thanks to Fernando Sor, these divided folks can move, in my mind, from "sore separate" to "soar together."

Love and Hate

Love and hate are opposites, and thus, like all opposites, they go together.

Thus, it is "reasonable" that behind the secular hatred of religion is love; behind religious hatred of the secular is love?

And is the same true in the political divide—i.e., that behind the hatred Trump is love, and behind the MAGA hatred of "liberals" is love?

Just because you kill them, that doesn't mean you don't love them (though, as an extreme solution, killing is not a good way to go).

Wednesday, June 7, 2023

Etymology is my love, and words are my passion. Feeling both combines intellect and sound, mind and emotion.

Etymos is the truth, real and meaningful.

To move on is to forget about the old life, or at least remember it as belonging to someone else. (It was once me, but not anymore.)

Thursday, June 8, 2023
Vibrational Mail

I want to be an artist again.

Today I began a new choreo for "The Entertainer," by Scott Joplin. First one in months.

The suffering-life attitude has run its many-year course. I sense it coming to a close. Get used to feeling better, even good: positive life direction, solid personal guidance, and an artist's loving of life.

Paradoxically, imprisoned in loves, bound in purity to my miracle schedule, brings me freedom. Without such bound-aries, disorganization wins; I become a slave to chaos.

But now I'm back to running, and yoga, Hebrew Torah studies, etymology with history, and Torah guitar.

What's Torah guitar? Healing humans through my guitar playing; bringing soothing and inner peace; curing loneliness. I start by thinking of others and focus on sending healing vibrations when I play. It's vibrational mail. All I have to do is imagine it into being, it being long-distance prayers in musical form. *Tikkun olam.*

Why not be a healer? Isn't that the best? Use my skills as instruments to orchestrate healing events.

Friday, June 9, 2023
Sin and Atonement

What is a *sin?*
Removal, I would say, from the source of life.
How does one sin?
A primary vehicle is lack of focus.
For me, that is a daily sin. My mind wanders, not only every day, but every hour, even every few minutes. So sin, removal from the source of life, is my constant companion.
Atonement, *at-one-ment*, means being at one.
(Repentance is the same. Here the punishment is regret.)
When I'm focused, I'm at one, united. Sacrifice means giving something up, usually in exchange for something better. I sacrifice the desired object of my wandering mind, namely, my distraction, for a straight-and-narrow focus on something better. For me this would mainly be guitar, folk dance, writing, study, exercise, and miracle-schedule events. It also means family, friends, business.
Monkey mind is the problem.

Saturday, June 10, 2023
Sound Folks

According to Karl Marx and dialectical materialism, opposites clash, and then a synthesis is created that transforms those opposites into something different, almost a higher union. So opposites attract and merge into something new.

Of course things are almost always polluted through guidance by the deceived. Under the illusion of doing what's right, people have killed each other in the name of both Communism and God. Whether the illusion is secular or religious doesn't seem to matter.

Sunday, June 11, 2023
United Abyss and Sky: The Ultimate Folk Dance Vision

Imagine me a Torah scholar! On one level, it is a total break from my Communist past. On another, a higher one, it is a total *union* with that past, bringing together, in a dialectical manner, both Communist and capitalist, left and right, by merging, synthesizing two opposites into a grand new whole, a qualitative leap. Karl Marx, Engels, Moses, Jesus, Einstein, Beethoven, all the heroes in my life would be proud.

Uniting all into one artistic whole would be quite a feat. It's not even that big a deal, since I just took a tiny step forward. With that step, I walked off the cliff into the abyss. But this time, just as I began to drop, saw the sky above and began to fly.

I picked up my guitar with new Torah vision in mind. A post-Covid Zohar shining. How about making "Alhambra" the new Torah Vision? Would this be orthodox guitar playing? Why not?

Play guitar, say, with an ultimate folk dance vision in mind. Combine the arts in one sky—political friends and foes, too, all trembling (tremoloing) in one big "Alhambra."

Monday, June 12, 2023

A good service to others would be to publish and advertise my latest journal, and all the older books, too. Do it not for ego but for service.

Could I do that? A totally new motivation source would be *service to others,* a Torah good-in-itself. The "I" would become beside the point. I don't know if I should, or even could, do this. I need ego satisfaction and love.

But I sure would like to find a good reason to publish and push my books.

Dialectical Truth and Coffee

Here's the dialectical truth: Love unifies the opposites, merges the warring factions. Just because you may need to eviscerate and destroy your enemies doesn't mean you can't love them. And sometimes, if you love them, you may not even need to eviscerate and destroy them. You might just go out for coffee.

Tuesday, June 13, 2023
Torah Scholar Vision

After my Monday night folk dance class, my legs ache. After the joy and ecstasy of a great night of dancing, my body feels totally destroyed. But something has changed. Although I still feel pain, frailty, discomfort, depression, and discouragement, I'm now taking all these miseries for granted, dealing with them more "in passing." I'm accepting their existence simply as part of my psyche. I'm paying less, or little, attention to them and moving on.

On to what? Miracle-schedule stuff, my new Torah life.

This word "Torah" still make me uncomfortable. By using it, applying it to myself, will I become a crazy Hasid? These folks are so off-the-wall: Look how they dress, act, and think. *Ugh,* but also *wow!* Much of me—nay, *most* of me—loves their craziness, their wild passion, how they dare to stand apart from society, announcing their distance with crazy clothes. How exotic.

But how can I square this feeling of attraction with my secular upbringing? Well, perhaps my teenage vision is the answer. In those days, I envisioned myself sitting in the attic at a small wooden desk illuminated by one lonely floor lamp. I sat there for hours, days, like a bearded Hasidic Einstein, timelessly studying the secrets of the universe.

I've had this dream since my teenage years. I still have it. Perhaps that is my life vision. I've always loved the dream, seen it as the height of existence. To study and learn: What could be better?

Saturday, June 17, 2023
Stock Market Trading and Love

Why do I keep on trading stocks? It's not for the money, although that is the marker. It's simply to win (and lose, too). It's just like getting checks for tour registrations in the mail. When I receive them, I jump for joy because it shows, proves, that God loves me. It's the same for me with trading stocks: When they go up, I win. When I win, I feel like God loves me. And love is very important to me—a vital source of spiritual food, nourishment of my core. I want and need this proof. Every day I need to know God loves me.

Of course, I realize this is totally twisted and not even right, an absurdly personal view of the meaning of love. But so what? That's what I have needed—until, I hope, now.

I hope it will deepen my grasp of stock trading, and I will somehow "learn" to stop it.

I know it's a waste of time. I make no money; I mostly lose it. And that is being *kind* to myself.

But I do it anyway, rationalizing my actions as best I can, trying to win and find meaning in winning.

Is there a better way for me to find love? Everyone, including me, believes there is. But will I ever act on this belief?

I'm looking to outside events for proof of love. Yet we have no control over outside events, only over our own attitudes or inner events.

The search to find love, of and from God, outside the self is frustrating and fruitless. Such love is an inner thing, and can only be found permanently within.

Does permanent love actually reside within? The way of faith would answer "Yes." If I do as well, am I confident my love does?

What's the difference between faith and confidence?

Confidence feels like an inner thing, while faith connects to the outer world. Faith in confidence, confidence in faith: A bit of a mess to connect them. But such is the drama of life.

Confrontation

Deep in my heart I know that direct confrontation is not my way. I'm simply bad at it. My immediate reaction to direct confrontation is the feeling that I will lose. Not a good way to start. But by pulling back, I get time to think. What's the best way to handle, to deal with, this? I look around, then try figuring out away to subtly influence the situation by entering through the back door. I like the back-door approach. It's cagey, smart, and strategic.

Monday, June 19, 2023
Reordering of Priorities: A New Look at Writing

All the old "fame and fortune" reasons for writing fell away during Covid.

But I see writing "The Right Step" as an end-of-the-day reward, a gift of pleasure. Such writing can be my dessert adventure into the crazy, off-the-wall, *Finnegans Wake, Mad Shoes*, free and wild life.

But at the *end* of the day, not the beginning.

Jump-Start My Day with a Business Bang!

This starts with an attack rather than monastic retreat. It reverses all my former, pre-Covid priorities. Rather than miracle-schedule practices, which are all inner-oriented, I begin my day by grabbing my sword, charging out the gate of my castle across the moat bridge and into the world with a bang, energized and wide awake.

Then, after the wars of business are over, done, finished, lost or won, I can stop, sit down, and relax with the cool beer of writing.

Tuesday, June 20, 2023
Flirting with the Devil

What is evil? Of course, there is *grand* evil, but I'm talking about *little* evil, namely the devil within. For me, it's about losing focus. First wandering off the path, then falling off the cliff.

The path to no sin is straight and sticky. No question about it. But the shut-up, just-do-it path is *so* hard to follow. Is flirting with the devil fun, a sport, a turn-on, part of our nature? Is the challenge worth the effort?

Thursday, June 22, 2023
A Reason to Play Guitar

This morning started without incident. I played guitar, but for no reason. It's part of the straight-and-narrow. A commandment.

It must be done.

Why? I don't *know* why. Call it an obligation. I was given a talent. I therefore have to use it. I'm in training for an indefinite future.

As for guitar, I do need to calm the frightened crowd, relax an audience, cast a spell over it with the *magic wand of my thumb.*

So that's my reason to play guitar. Not to excite an audience, but to settle the wild and fear-filled beasts within. Of course, I include myself among them. It's what drove the Baroque—a very difficult time to be alive in, a time of endless catastrophe, with impending political and religious chaos, rampant disease, poor hygiene, and a desperate daily struggle to put food in your mouth, find shelter, make ends meet. . .and out of that came Pachelbel and Bach and Telemann, and transcendent music that made sense of it all.

Saturday, June 24, 2023

It feels like a big deal, but I don't want to make a big deal out of it. Something has happened with my guitar and the pieces I play. It's finally becoming an instrument, *my* instrument.

This scares and embarrasses me. Mostly embarrasses. To take God into my playing, to play for Him, with Him, through Him, to become His instrument, to directly say God's name, embarrasses me. I feel Him, but I dare not *say* Him, speak His name.

No question, such a direct relationship with Him would remove all performing fears.

But what would Ma, Uncle Willie, my family, and all the others say? I would become, in their eyes—to say nothing of my own as well—a heretic, traitor to the secular, religion-is-the-opiate-of-the-people cause. Plus everyone knows that Karl Marx is the real god, along with his saints like Stalin, Engels, Trotsky for a while, etc. I would be seen as a religious nut, off the wall, truly crazy but note: *artist* crazy, that's okay, but *religious* crazy, that's not.

Well, truth is, I *believe* in crazy, and certainly all my life have believed in artistic craziness. What, after all is *Mad Shoes* all about? Although I am not a religious nut, I am an artistic nut, a beauty nut, or as Keats might say, a truth-and- beauty nut.

But a religious nut and an artistic nut are really the same subversive lunatic. Only the words are different, using different names for similar feelings. Politics belongs to the lower world. Truth-Beauty-Religion-Art belong to the higher.

I need to live in both. But as I travel in the lower world, I have to as much as possible remember the upper one.

From Alhambra to Elhambra

Al-hambra: *Al* means "the" in Arabic; *hambra* means "red."
El-hambra: *El* is God in Hebrew; *hambra* again means "red." (Or does it? Perhaps it symbolizes blood.)
Total Thumb equals total faith in God. (He'll take care of the fingers in His own time.) Uniting God and guitar playing, and vice versa, is Jewish guitar playing at its best. Connecting with the Higher Forces. Moving from "Alhambra" to "Elhambra."

Sunday, June 25, 2023

Sparks are not flying today, and dullness is settling in. Is it fear—of flying? I just crossed my running limit, went too fast for too long, and got scared. I had come too far and might hurt myself. And it fits perfectly: My inner demon of discouragement usually appears after my victories.

What to do? Plough on, in spite of it, because of it. Bypass it. Does this quivering mean turn or recommit? Both are good. Synthesis is the only answer. Merge these two good but opposite thoughts. How?

Recommit to creativity! Do *both*. But as I do, loosen, widen the straight-and-narrow path.

As a start, try combining Jewish guitar with Torah flow.

It was all together, connected, purposeful and heading in the right direction on the path for one glorious week. But now the week is over, done, successful, finished. I'm at the end of this chapter. My stomach is rumbling as I step once again, into the "Now what?" unknown.

Monday, June 26, 2023
Clouds

Dark clouds, storms clouds, light clouds, large clouds, small clouds, all clouds, but clouds coming and going, arising and passing, all kinds of shapes and sizes, strong and weak, are a fact of life.

What to do about them? How to handle them?

To stay on the path in spite of the clouds is best. Take cover if I need to, do whatever I have to do to survive, but keep on the rocky road; focus on the known good and the activities that feed me.

Good Sportsmanship

Perhaps a positive attitude toward fighting the dark cloud might help. See darkness as a twisted angel friend, something to struggle against, to compete with, in order to learn how to fight better and discover inner powers. How can I know my strengths and weaknesses without opposition to test me?

Isn't it better to appreciate, even thank, your opponent? especially if he, she, or it is a good one? Who can better teach you how to fight, know your best self, and become a better winner or loser?

Good sportsmanship is a worthy goal. I like how it creates a positive attitude toward winning or losing. It's a strong psychological tool to use. . .and it works even against a dark cloud.

Tuesday, June 27, 2023

I'm reclaiming my artistic soul. But this time it feels different, more than that. I have just absorbed Torah guitar. Its biblical shadow has floated away, like clouds in the sky, which, after raining on me, left growth effects after their watering work was done.

Wednesday, June 28, 2023
Loosening the Reins

Here's a unexpected self-definition: As a CEO, I'm having a lot of fun. My social director self is blossoming. I'm dropping the pressure of being an artist. As a CEO, there's really nothing I can't handle, as opposed to the impossible perfection goals of the classical guitar, where I am striving, spinning my wheels on a treadmill, and never arriving home.

Artistic ventures will become my relaxing hobby.

Fun Spot Life

Having fun is victory over the contrary forces of life. I'd like to bring some of it into my art. (Continue on the path, and it might happen naturally.) What a wonderful place to be. Once achieved, I can die having fun!

But not yet, please. I'm just getting started on Earth. Why stop now? Make it eternal play. The secret classical-guitar-playing spot I've been trying to find that pours through my right index and is fed by my right-hand hypothenar muscles is the *fun spot*. How to live there? It sleeps at night but forgets to wake up in the morning.

Reviving it is my daily goal.

Living in it is where my Covid era (period) search ends.

Thursday, June 29, 2023
Giving Up Expectations

I'm having a touch of tour disgust (and anger).

I hope I'm sick of them and ready to move on.

Today is about giving up my tour expectations, bringing them down to zero, and starting over. It's a slow, difficult, painful, but cleansing descent.

I wonder if expectations, which are always untrue and a form of sin, since they "predict" the future rather than anticipate it, come at the end of energy cycles and are a way of holding onto the original energy impetus, which feels so good! As such, they signal the end or dying off of the energy cycle.

I'm there now, at the end.

It's time for me to take a break, I think. I have the upcoming six days of the July 4 weekend.

With this new approach to guitar, business, and life, the whole Alhambra tremolo problem and general questions about whether my playing should be slow, fast, or any other way, disappear.

Now it makes absolutely no difference whether I play slow, fast, medium, or some other as yet undiscovered way.

About the Author

Jim Gold brings color to his worlds as a folk dance teacher, choreographer, musician, writer, tour organizer, and president of his travel company, Jim Gold International Folk Dance Tours.

His welcoming personality and enthusiasm for life inspires his folk dance students and travelers alike. He's also a classical and folk guitarist. His one-man show has appeared on TV and in schools and universities across the USA.

He has written ten books, many of which chronicle his varied life.

www.ingramcontent.com/pod-product-compliance
Lightning Source LLC
Chambersburg PA
CBHW071714090426
42738CB00009B/1765